Clean, & Green Reliable

By Douglas J. Plucknette and Christopher A. Colson

RELIABILITY®
WEB.COM

Clean, Green, and Reliable

Douglas J. Plucknette and Christopher A. Colson

ISBN 978-0-9832258-2-9

Publisher: Terrence O'Hanlon
Layout and design: Nicola Behr

For information: Reliabilityweb.com
www.reliabilityweb.com
PO Box 60075, Ft. Myers, FL 33906
Toll Free: 888-575-1245 | Phone: 239-333-2500
E-mail: customerservice@reliabilityweb.com

10   9   8   7   6   5   4   3   2

Let me start by saying this book is not about global warming, the melting of the polar ice caps, and the death of mankind.

It is also not an ultraconservative rant about former Vice President Al Gore, liberals, actors, or Hollywood.

It's a book about common sense.

About doing the right thing.

It's about making more with less and each of us doing our part to make our manufacturing companies more reliable, energy-efficient, cost-effective, and competitive.

It is also about being a steward to God's earth, knowing that what we leave behind we leave to our children and to their children.

Let's forget all the politics and all the people who get paid to stir the pot and fog the issues.

This is a book about being smart, being responsible, and being successful.

Book Dedication

by Doug Plucknette

would like to begin by thanking my friend and colleague Chris Colson for his huge part in making this book become reality. While this book started as a result in my interest in equipment reliability, how improving reliability improves energy efficiency and the environment, my goal was to provide a sound, easy-to-read book that addressed what we can do as business owners, managers, and reliability engineers to improve the reliability of our assets, improve energy efficiency, and lower the cost of doing business. I think I had several good ideas regarding the layout and content of the book, but what I lacked was knowledge and experience on the electrical side of our business. Chris more than filled this role. Chris has a degree in electrical engineering and has worked directly with manufacturing companies around the country, helping them to improve energy efficiency. When it comes to the world of consulting, I am not easily impressed; having been in this business for nearly 15 years, I have worked with some extremely bright and talented people, and most of them aren't afraid to let you know how bright and talented they are! Chris is at the top of this list, easygoing, calm, extremely intelligent, and best of all a humble guy who works his tail off to make things better for his family and our company. Chris, thanks for helping me pull this thing out of the scrap heap and make our vision become a reality we both can be proud of.

I would also like to thank "Allied Al" Othmer for his help in providing most of the pictures in this book, as well as his involvement in the case studies section. There is no one more passionate about energy efficiency than Al. As Chris and I were researching several chapters we would often call Al to get his take on what the reality is in regard to the claims we had all read in ads and on the Internet. Al's hands-on, real-life experience was a great resource for us. He really understands the business of equipment reliability, energy efficiency, and the business case for change.

I can quite honestly say that were it not for South Carolina State Senator Paul Campbell and Allied owner and president John Schultz, this book would not be complete today. Two years ago I made the mistake of telling John that I had a good idea for another book; he listened to what I had to say and said, "I like it—when will you be done?"

About a year later John introduced me to Al, and from that point on the two of them asked me every few months, "How's it coming? When will Chris and you be finished with the book? This is a very important subject, and we have been talking to a lot of people who are excited to read it!"

Well guys… It's done!

Thanks to the nearly 200 people who have joined the Reliability is Green group on LinkedIn. While this is not a huge number in comparison to some of the LinkedIn groups, it is the original supporters who mean the most. I have a good idea this thing is going to catch on over the next few years, and I look forward to our future discussions.

Last but not least, to my wife, Leslie, I thanked her first in my first book and I am thanking her last in this one because my world begins and ends with her and the life we created together. While I have told her a thousand times, I don't think she has any idea what an example she has been for me and how I am better at what I do today because of her. My wife has to be one of the best teachers in the country—and if you don't believe me, just ask the children who have had her and the parents of these kids how she changes kids' lives. While schools all around the country have focused on test results, my wife in all her years of teaching has focused on teaching in a way that makes children enjoy both school and learning. Here's how she puts it: "If I can teach them to love reading, they will love to read the rest of their lives; if I can teach them to love math, they will continue to love math as well." She has taught some of the toughest kids, and year in and year out it is no surprise to me that her students continue to excel.

Leslie, it was your style and passion I used when I began facilitating and instructing RCM, and guess what I found out? That if you make learning about and performing RCM fun, people will continue to do RCM.

Imagine that!

Doug Plucknette

Book Dedication

by Chris Colson

I would like to start by thanking my friend and colleague Doug Plucknette. I have had the pleasure of working with Doug over the past four years and have learned an enormous amount, not only in regard to equipment reliability but also life lessons—reflected by the way Doug handles himself in an array of situations. Doug has been the kind of colleague who is always open and willing to teach, debate, learn, and resolve issues to improve upon "the way things have always been done." Doug is one of the most practical and professional people I know. Thank you, Doug, for including me in this endeavor; it has been an enjoyable learning experience.

I too would like to thank Al Othmer ("Allied Al") for his help in providing an abundance of material used throughout this book. It takes less than two minutes speaking with Al to realize and feel his passion for energy efficiency and conservation. Al is a consummate professional and constantly searches for real-life solutions to implement for our clients and improve their "way of doing business." It has been a pleasure working with Al, and I am looking forward to many more years of the same.

I would like to thank the many other individuals from the Allied Reliability team for their support and continued hard work making Allied the best PdM company in the world. It is a special feeling to be surrounded by so many passionate experts in the reliability industry. Every single day is full of opportunities to learn, expand, challenge, and push the envelope. There are a few colleagues I would like to single out and thank for their assistance and support during the research for this book, including Hans De Kegel, James Sawyer, Sid Lane, James Wheeler, Jason Langhorne, Mark Geller, Tim Weilbaker, Steve Malec, John Trulli, Dustin Morris, Carey Repasz, and Chris Klosterman. Of course, I would also like to thank two of the best owners one could ever hope to work for: John Langhorne and John Schultz. These two gentlemen truly understand how to encourage, support, and empower their employees to create an environment that is truly effective and enjoyable. Without their dedication and constant support, this would not have been possible.

I would also like to thank Senator Paul Campbell for his willingness to be involved with this book and for his insightful thoughts in the Forward. It has been a true pleasure knowing and working with him.

My last and greatest thanks are for my wife and best friend, Beth, whose love, guidance, encouragement, and patience will always be treasured. Without a doubt, you are the glue that holds our family together. We have three beautiful daughters, Mara, Macy, and Abby, who we so dearly love and enjoy. Thank you for your tireless efforts on my behalf and on behalf of our children. Your loyalty and dedication have been steadfast and complete. Your love and compassion have been unwavering. Beth, you are unbelievable, and I am eternally grateful to have you in my life.

Chris Colson

Table of Contents

Chapter 1: Precision Alignment and Balancing............................1

We address the topics of alignment and balancing in general, discussing the known effects that the two have on energy efficiency. How much more energy as a percentage will be consumed by a motor that is out of alignment, or by a fan that is out of balance?

Chapter 2: Ultrasonic Leak Detection 5

In this chapter we address the topic of leak detection and provide general information on how this technology can be used to return massive ROIs with the savings from detecting compressed air, gas, and steam leaks.

Chapter 3: Electric Motor Reliability 13

We examine motor efficiency and reliability, utilizing techniques such as Motor Circuit Analysis and Power Quality Analysis to determine the health of the motor (i.e., the condition of the winding, stator, etc.). We consider common design problems and the use of high-efficiency motors. Motor PMs come in here as well: clean motors with proper airflow are just one example.

power is more reliable and efficient. We analyze specific electrical failure modes that affect reliability and efficiency.

This chapter addresses steam and condensate systems and the potential energy waste that results from unreliability. We introduce some simple operating and maintenance tasks that can be performed to maintain reliable and efficient steam and condensate systems.

We take a look at two fantastic case studies where projects that were aimed at improving equipment reliability also resulted in significant improvement in energy efficiency.

Our final chapter provides an inside look at Allied Reliability's approach to energy management with a foundation in equipment reliability.

Foreword

by Paul G. Campbell Jr.
Senator, South Carolina

The metals smelting industry is one of the largest energy users in the world. As president of the Southeast region for Alcoa Primary Metals, I saw power bills for smelters exceeding $150 million per year for a single smelter, with some months costing as much as $15 million at one plant. These are staggering sums costing as much as a third of the entire cost to produce primary aluminum. In fact, aluminum's highest manufacturing expense is power. Consider that a 1 mV decrease in our energy usage translated into an annual savings of $20,000 or more. Suffice it to say that like other Alcoa executives, I became an energy expert. I spent a career dissecting production processes in an effort to continuously improve our energy use profile. We scrutinized any and every process that used energy. What we learned is that before you can get truly green and lean, you have to embed reliability engineering into your manufacturing operations. So what does that mean? Everyone wants to be green and lean and save energy, but how exactly is that done? How is reliability engineering incorporated into an industrial plant? The answers to these questions are provided within these pages, for a wide range of industrial venues.

For those new to the concept, reliability engineering is a methodology to maximize the performance of a given component at a given rate, time, and set of circumstances. In other words, reliability approaches aim to leverage the function, time, and cost variables of an industrial system for maximum return on investment. It's a money saver that happens to do a lot of other good things. As a science, reliability engineering is practically new. It began in the early 1990s, when industries first developed protocols for reducing maintenance overhead and extending the useful life of their equipment assets in response to increasingly competitive pressures from the global market.

In a very real sense, the reliability domain was a green enterprise from the start. The act of extending a product's or system's useful life is a fundamental green practice. But the earliest reliability measures tended to target the bottom line alone. The current practice evolved to address other beneficial outcomes, including reducing adverse events, reducing demand maintenance, and saving capital expenditures. Industries' perceptions of benefits also evolved. As recently as 1995, many industry leaders viewed reduced energy costs as merely an incidental benefit, whereas today the seeds of green energy savings fall on very fertile ground around industry boardrooms. People are becoming aware of the power of reliability. As well they should, considering that corporate pledges and demonstrations for the responsible stewardship of our planet's shared resources are today's social, operational, marketing, and public relations imperatives. The good news is that reliability practices help everyone, and they unanimously improve every single facet of industrial manufacturing processes. A few of the holistic returns include:

- **Manufacturing**—Reliability is the cornerstone for green and lean manufacturing. Overall equipment effectiveness (OEE) reduces run time to make product. Less run time reduces energy consumption and compensation. Less scrap and rework mean less spent energy. Reduced product variation translates into gains in market share and better utilization and improved quality, equaling greater value for the customer.

- **Energy Profile**—Reliability processes reduce energy expenditures in all production processes. Run time is optimized with fewer stops and starts. Energy losses resulting from poor alignment, out-of-balance issues, and poor contact points and electrical joints are reduced. Premature failure of hardware and equipment is prevented. Fewer support staff and utilities are needed, such as additional personnel to address steam leaks and boiler run time and maintenance. Process interruptions related to refrigeration and hydraulic-system down time are minimized. Reduced power demand premiums reduce dependence on power plants.

- **Productivity**—Fewer process interruptions increase the productivity of operators and crafts people; increase the morale, time on project, and *esprit de corps* among operators and maintenance staff; and improve the retention of employees.

- **Market/Sales**—Market share improves as manufacturing processes become more efficient, customer appreciation increases, and industrial segment leadership develops. As the bottom line improves, market share expands, as does the need for more jobs.

- **Capital Costs**—Less power demand translates into lower capital expenditures. Lower capital costs, in turn, reduce the demand for energy raw materials.

- **Safety**—As reliability profiles go up, safety and lost time instances decrease.

- **Community**—Better community relations and corporate image.

Industries should ask themselves, "What am I losing?" "Can I reduce wasted expenses from 25% to 5%?" "What is my hidden plant?" Your hidden plant is your true capacity. It is the amount of production capacity underutilized because of process inefficiencies. Instead of building a new plant, reliability engineering helps you postpone that capital expense. The science has caught on to make this option viable.

Having more units with the same hardware further spreads fixed cost, driving down unit cost and both improving competitive positions and mitigating (or at least delaying) needs for new capacity. Reliability is indeed the new frontier in manufacturing. Just think: If you are not adopting reliability concepts, your competitors are. This should be a scary thought!

The authors of *Clean, Green, and Reliable* are the some of the world's foremost authorities on the growing science of reliability engineering. Doug Plucknette is a field expert; creator of RCM Blitz™; author of *Reliability Centered Maintenance using RCM Blitz*, a valuable model affecting asset health; and has been in the maintenance and reliability field since 1981. Chris Colson graduated from the University of Louisville with a B.S. in electrical engineering, has served on an academic advisory board, has particular expertise in industrial automation and energy conservation, and has been in the maintenance and reliability field since 1994.

The book includes a comprehensive array of testing techniques and manufacturing systems that can be used by company owners, executives, managers, engineers, supervisors, technicians, mechanics, electricians, and operators. Chapters 1 and 2 are overviews of precision alignment/balancing and ultrasonic leak detection, respectively. Chapters 3 through 10 are discussions of reliability issues associated with the following specific systems: electric motors, HVAC/exhaust, air/gas conveyance, compressed air, refrigeration, hydraulic, electric power, and steam and condensates. Chapter 11 is a presentation of two actual case studies, and Chapter 12 is a description of the industry expert and leader in reliability engineering.

Read, study, apply, and become more competitive. Reliability concepts work!

Paul G. Campbell Jr.
Senator, South Carolina

Preface

How Equipment Reliability Delivers Low-Cost, Energy-Efficient Assets at Plants Around the World

by Doug Plucknette and Chris Colson

first became interested in manufacturing reliability nearly 20 years ago working as a maintenance mechanic who had a personal interest in improving the reliability of individual assets by searching through our maintenance history for areas where we were spending the most time and money with regard to emergency/demand work orders. Using the history we had in our database, we used the 80/20 approach to identify the 20% of our assets where we spent nearly 80% of our maintenance budget. Once we identified a system or asset to work on, we would use a cause-map or root cause analysis to identify the potential causes of our equipment failures. Understanding these causes, we would then look to identify potential redesigns to eliminate or reduce the frequency of equipment failures.

In working on these problems and identifying solutions as a group, we also began to recognize the power behind understanding the relationship between cause and effect, noting that a single cause could have several effects and any given effect could also have several causes. We also noticed in finding solutions to the causes of many equipment failures that the impact of these solutions reached far beyond the measures of equipment reliability.

While the benefits of equipment reliability are most noted for reducing the cost of maintenance, the benefits of reliable assets reach far beyond the cost of eliminating emergency and demand maintenance. In wrapping up each project, we highlighted the benefits and savings derived to drive home the point that equipment reliability would deliver more than a reduction in maintenance costs. For each project we would report the following information:

- Overall Equipment Effectiveness (OEE) in the months before the project and following implementation.
- Number of maintenance man-hours dedicated to maintaining the asset 12 months before the start of the project and again in the months following implementation.
- Parts costs before and after the project.
- Energy usage/costs in the 12 months before the start of the project and in the months following implementation.

Nearly every time our teams reported this information in meetings to management, I found it interesting that someone would comment that the savings and increase in productivity were significant but the energy savings were insignificant:

"As a company we generate our own utilities, so the 25% reduction in energy usage for this asset will not result in a cost savings to the company. Unless the savings were significant enough to warrant the shutdown of one of our boilers or turbines, it has no impact on the company bottom line."

"Thanks for the effort, but next time leave the energy piece out of the equation!"

Fast-forward 15 years and things are a little different. Most of the MBAs I used to work for have had to go find employment someplace else. It would seem that for most, all they learned in graduate school was to nod their head yes after our former CEO demanded they do something stupid.

Simon says, "Nod your head yes!"

I believe one would now get a totally different response should he or she be able to reduce energy consumption at any manufacturing facility. Regardless of one's beliefs about global warming, reducing energy consumption is the right thing to do—especially when we can show that this reduction in energy consumption is a by-product of improved equipment/manufacturing reliability.

As a reliability engineer and consultant, I find it exciting that nearly every major company in the world includes pages about energy efficiency and environmental responsibility on its corporate website. I'm excited because I know that reliable systems, processes, and assets are both energy-efficient and environmentally responsible.

The idea to write this book came out of some discussions I had with Terry O'Hanlon about my purchase of the domain name Reliabilityisgreen.com, an idea I had while writing the *RCM Blitz* book. Terry and I have both experienced how improved reliability can have a positive impact on energy efficiency, and it was Terry who had the idea for this book. While we both have experienced this relationship between manufacturing reliability and energy efficiency, the true experts who can answer the questions of what we need to do, why it works, and what results we should expect will be key contributors to this text. With this information and a few real-life case studies on how equipment reliability improves energy efficiency, we hope to enlighten the masses on how reliability delivers energy efficiency.

As the project moved forward and Chris Colson came on board, Chris and I started researching and reading about the various reliability tools and methods that made general claims regarding energy savings. While some of these claims have been substantiated, there are others for which the jury is still out. The most popular claim of energy savings is "up to 20%." If you read that some device can deliver up to a 20% reduction in energy costs or a 20% improvement in energy efficiency, use a bit of common sense and ask for a case study or client testimonial. If there is one thing I know about manufacturing managers, it is that they will not release fudged numbers to the public.

Chris and I wanted this book to be different from the other books aimed at business in regard to energy savings. I bet I can find at least 20 books that talk about reducing energy usage by upgrading the building lighting, windows, and office thermostats. With plenty of this information available, we wanted to write about some common systems and technologies where if businesses focused some time and effort, they would see a quick return on investment and an improvement in reliability.

While this effort has taken nearly two years of our time, we are pleased with the results and believe you will be as well.

Doug Plucknette

Chapter 1

Precision Alignment and Balancing

A s I mentioned before, it was my background in improving maintenance and reliability that first got me interested in the idea that reliable manufacturing equipment is also energy-efficient equipment. Having seen proof over the years that precision alignment has a direct effect on the reliability and overall life of our rotating equipment, I made the assumption that precision alignment must have a similar impact on energy consumption. Therefore, I reasoned that a motor that is not properly aligned will use more power/energy than a motor that has been precision aligned. Common sense would tell you that rotation misalignment causes increased load on and vibration of the bearings—and that as load and vibration increases, the amount of energy required to turn the motor must also increase.

A motor that is not properly aligned will use more power/ energy than a motor that has been precision aligned.

As it turns out, proving this fact was more difficult than I expected.

I would estimate that in the past 15 years I have attended at least 60 maintenance and reliability conferences, and at each I spent a significant amount of time in the exhibition hall talking to various vendors who were selling products and services intended to improve equipment reliability. It was by talking with these vendors that I first believed I could find some good information regarding the effect that precision alignment has on energy consumption.

My collection of information from companies that sell precision alignment tools included the following claims:

Easy-Laser® states that good alignment of motors results in a 1% overall energy savings and a savings of 5–10% for sheave/pulley alignment. This information is connected to a customer case study that recognized an annual energy savings of 140,000 euros. *(Ref. 1)*

Ludeca Inc. case studies show that properly aligned v-belt drives are 97% efficient and poorly aligned v-belt drives lose as much as 10% efficiency. *(Ref. 2)*

Other manufacturers of precision alignment tools and companies that sell precision alignment training and services made claims in the range of 1–20% improvement in energy efficiency, but only Easy-Laser® and Ludeca included actual case studies to support this information.

With this information in hand, I set out to find other supporting documents and case studies about the impact that precision alignment has on energy efficiency. The following information from the University of Tennessee and the Department of Energy (DOE) did not help to prove my assumption that proper alignment improves energy efficiency.

In a case study performed by J.W. Hines, S. Jesse, and A. Edmondson at the University of Tennessee Maintenance and Reliability Center, and at the Oak Ridge Center for Electric Machinery System Testing, two 50 horsepower (hp) three-phase motors were tested to define the relationship between motor misalignment and motor efficiency using a precision dynamometer and four different manufacturers' flexible couplings. The motors were operated under full load condition, first under precision aligned conditions (0 offset and 0 angularity) and then misaligned to various degrees.

The results of this part of the research show no measurable change in motor efficiency related to motor shaft misalignment when the tested couplings were operated within the manufacturer's recommended range. Power consumption and output remained steady regardless of motor position. (Data showed efficiency change of less than .01%.) However, these results in no way reduce the importance of precise motor alignment. Other motor performance characteristics, such as vibration and coupling and bearing temperature, were measured and showed notable increases with increased misalignment. These traits are all related to increased bearing loads, and the findings suggest that misalignment reduces the life span and reliability of motors and their associated components. *(Ref. 3)*

The DOE's Industrial Technologies Program reports in a Motor Systems tip sheet, "While misalignment has no measurable effect on motor efficiency, correct shaft alignment ensures the smooth, efficient transmission of power from the motor to the driven equipment. Incorrect alignment occurs when the centerlines of the motor and the driven equipment shafts are not in line with each other. Misalignment produces excessive vibration, noise, coupling and bearing temperature increases, and premature bearing or coupling failure." *(Ref. 4)*

Trying to make sense of it all, let's be optimistic and say that it is entirely possible that improving alignment of rotating equipment motors' shafts sheaves/pulleys could net your company a return in energy efficiency of 1%. A plant that was running a number of electric motors that totaled 7,000 kW and ran the motors for 6,000 hours per year would use 42 million kWh of power. A 1% improvement in energy efficiency would reduce its consumption by 42,000 kWh. So if this company were paying an average of 12 cents per kWh, its annual energy savings for proper alignment would total $50,400. Add this to the improvement in equipment reliability—which is far more significant—and we should now show a significant boost in reliability and costs.

The only provider that actually offered a calculation for determining potential savings through precision alignment was PdM Solutions of San Antonio, Texas. The following information is available on the company's web page:

Saving Energy Costs Through Precision Alignment

It has been reported that precision alignment can save power consumption by 1 to 3%. There is also a conflicting study report that finds no significant correlation between misalignment and machine efficiency. As well, there has been no study done indicating the energy savings for screw compressors used in refrigeration and process gas that have utilized precision alignment. However, it is not an overstatement that precision alignment can save energy consumption by reducing mechanical inefficiency. Below is a calculation for the annual dollar savings of a compressor with 350HP motor.

Yearly Savings = (Motor H.P. x 0.746) x (1/Efficiency) x Power Cost x Average Annual Operating Hour x % saving.

For 350 HP motor running 6000 annual operating hours in San Antonio, TX, yearly savings will be calculated as below.

Yearly Savings = (350 x 0.746) x (1/0.95) x $0.0613/kwh x 6000 x 0.02=$2,021/ yearly savings. (Ref. 5)

Remembering that, as stated in the opening chapter, energy efficiency is a by-product of reliability, in the case of precision alignment we perform this task to improve the reliability and life cycle of the rotating assets. Precision alignment of your rotating assets has proven time and time again to deliver reduced maintenance costs and improve reliability.

Precision alignment of rotating assets is a crucial element when it comes to maximizing equipment reliability and can improve the energy efficiency of these assets.

Reference Notes:

1. Easy-Laser®, http://www.damalini.com/Savings-example-1-467.aspx.

2. Bill Hillman, "Maintaining Belt Drives for Maximum Savings," *Maintenance Technology,* 2010, http://www.mt-online.com/mtsection/ 273-july2010/1551-maintaining-belt-drives-for-maximum-savings.html.

3. J.W. Hines, S. Jesse, and A. Edmondson, "Effects of Motor Misalignment on Rotating Machinery," Maintenance and Reliability Center, University of Tennessee.

4. Department of Energy, "Motor Systems Tip Sheet #4," 2005, http://www1.eere.energy.gov/industry/bestpractices/motors.html.

5. PdM Solutions of San Antonio Inc., http://pdmsa.com/service-alignment.html.

Chapter 2

Ultrasonic Leak Detection

When it comes to the learning, certification, and use of predictive maintenance technologies to improve equipment reliability and energy efficiency, airborne ultrasound technology is a guaranteed home run. While my hands-on experience and certifications with PdM technologies are extremely limited, the one technology with which I have personal field experience in use and application is airborne ultrasound.

Once thought to be a low-end predictive maintenance technology that could be used as a complementary addition to vibration analysis and infrared inspections, the airborne ultrasound tools have now found a firm and well-deserved place as a critical stand-alone technology that can be used to identify a wide variety of conditions that affect safety, reliability, and energy efficiency.

The airborne ultrasound technology listens and detects noise above the range of human hearing (12–20 kHz), and the term "ultrasonic" refers to the sound range above the human hearing range of 20 kHz. The portable airborne ultrasound tools use a transducer to detect and identify noise in the ultrasonic range with the understanding that the mechanical vibrations that can be interpreted as sound are able to travel through all forms of matter, including solids, liquids, and gases. The instrument allows the user to easily identify noise in the ultrasonic range as well as the direction and source of the noise.

Applications of Airborne Ultrasound and the Benefits of Each

Compressed Air Leak Detection: The most common application for airborne ultrasound is to detect leaks of compressed air that are not detectable within the human range of sound. The high frequencies generated by the air leaks are electronically translated down to the range of human hearing by a process called heterodyning, where they are heard through the headphones and viewed as intensity levels on the instrument display panel. By pointing at or scanning an area where compressed air is used, your technician can hear the ultrasonic sounds through headphones and determine the general location of the leak and then install the focus module to pinpoint the exact source of the leak. Once the source has been identified, a good airborne ultrasonic instrument such as the UE 10,000, the UE 15,000, or the SDT 270 will allow the user to determine the size of the leak as well as the associated energy loss. By developing formal routes to detect, identify, measure, tag, and repair leaks, your company will be able to very quickly improve the performance and efficiency of your compressed air system. In measuring each leak we can then upload the data from the instrument to software that totals your losses, using the cost of your electrical power, and identifies your potential energy savings when the leaks are repaired. It should be noted that the large majority of these leaks can be quickly repaired by your PdM technician and a tradesperson as the leaks are identified. The latest instrument also lets the user record the leak point and location in your plant into its route and photograph the leak point at the time it is identified and tagged. It should also be noted that just because you have performed your initial leak detection route and repaired your leaks, you should never assume that your system will never leak again. I typically recommend to customers performing RCM that they perform air leak routes on a quarterly basis.

Companies like UE Systems Inc. and SDT report that most companies who invest in their airborne ultrasonic instrument typically see a return on investment for the cost of the instrument, training, and certification of technicians within two months of application in air leak energy savings alone! To fully understand the potential energy savings recognized by companies that use airborne ultrasonic instruments to identify and eliminate air leaks, you should check out the case studies chapter of this book. *(Ref. 1)*

Compressed Gas Leak Detection: Nearly identical to the identification of compressed air leaks, compressed gas leaks can also be easily identified and eliminated by developing routine PdM routes. And as with the compressed air leaks, the software for your device can determine the amount of and potential losses from these leaks by applying the cost of the compressed gas. Depending on the different types and amount of compressed gases your company uses, the savings here can be significant.

Steam Trap Failures: When steam traps leak or fail, this can be extremely costly in terms of product quality, safety, and energy loss. There are great differences in the way particular steam traps work (for example, inverted bucket trap versus float and thermostatic trap). A quality airborne ultrasonic instrument makes it easy to adjust for these differences and readily determine operating conditions while steam traps are on-line.

By contacting the instrument probe to the piping both upstream and downstream of the steam trap and comparing the intensity levels, your technician can quickly make a determination regarding the operation of each trap. If the sound is louder downstream, the fluid is passing through. If the sound level is low, the trap is closed. Ultrasonic steam trap inspection is considered a "positive" test in that an operator can instantly identify sound quality and intensity differentials and thereby determine operating conditions accurately. The identification of failed steam traps should be an essential part of your PdM program. This is because failed traps can have varied effects and consequences for your business, and it is important to educate your tradespeople and operators about the importance of proper trap function.

Again as with the case of compressed air leaks, your company is going to want to develop routine steam trap testing routes that should be performed on a regular (quarterly) basis. Having repaired and/or replaced hundreds of steam traps in my career, I can assure you that using this instrument to identify failed steam traps will easily pay for the cost of the device, the technician's time to complete the routes, and the cost to repair the leaks. Despite what some might believe, steam is not cheap, the loss of condensate from your system is not insignificant, and failed steam traps are a big deal. In the past year I worked at a site that had so many steam and condensate leaks that their concrete pad that supports millions of dollars in assets had eroded to a point where they were having a difficult time holding precision alignment on their rotating assets. Add this to the significant cost of the lost steam and condensate, and we are looking at a company that is losing millions of dollars in lost production and energy.

So what are the potential benefits? Let's use the estimate that in a plant with no active steam trap testing and repair program, 50% of the traps are blowing steam. If the plant were to implement a quarterly inspection and corrective repair program, the amount of leaking traps could be reduced to less than 5%. Using a conservative example that the cost to generate steam is $8 per 1,000 pounds of steam, and that a single trap with a 3/32" orifice operating at 100 psi can lose 30 lbs. of steam each hour, we can determine that the total cost of lost steam for this single trap totals more than $2,000 per year in lost energy. (*Ref. 2*)

Electrical Panels: Ultrasound inspection may be performed at all voltages (low, medium, and high). When electrical apparatuses such as switchgear, transformers, insulators, or disconnects and splices fail, the results can be catastrophic. This is just as true in industrial plants as it is in the power transmission and distribution side. Electrical discharges such as arcing, tracking, or, in higher voltages, corona have the potential to create equipment failure and costly downtime. In addition, the problems of RFI and TVI affect our valuable communication networks. If left undetected, these conditions can become a source of an arc flash incident, which can cause severe injury or death. Arcing, tracking, and corona produce ultrasound and are detected with an airborne ultrasound instrument.

How Ultrasonic Electrical Detection Works

Arcing, tracking, and corona all produce ionization, which disturbs the surrounding air molecules. The instrument detects high frequency sounds produced by these emissions and translates them (via heterodyning) down into the audible ranges. The specific sound quality of each type of emission is heard in headphones while the intensity of the signal is observed on a display panel. These sounds may be recorded and analyzed through ultrasound spectral analysis software for a more accurate diagnosis. Normally, electrical equipment should be silent, although some equipment, such as transformers, may produce a constant 60-cycle hum or some steady mechanical noises. These should not be confused with the erratic, sizzling, uneven, and popping sound of an electrical discharge.

Detection Method

Essentially, as in generic leak detection, the area of inspection is scanned starting at a high sensitivity level. To determine the location of the emission, reduce the sensitivity and follow the sound to the loudest point. If it is not possible to remove covers, plates, or doors, scan around the seams and vent slots. Any potentially damaging discharges should be detected.

For a more accurate diagnosis, ultrasound spectral analysis software helps identify sound patterns related to electrical emissions through spectral (FFT) and time series screens. Some of the more advanced instruments have on-board sound recording, while others have on-board spectral analysis screens to help provide a diagnosis on the spot. (*Ref. 3*)

Bearings

Inspection of mechanical equipment with ultrasonic instruments has many advantages. Ultrasound inspection provides early warning of bearing failure, detects lack of lubrication, prevents over-lubrication, and can be used on all bearing speeds (high, medium, and low). In addition, since ultrasound is a high-frequency short-wave signal, it is possible to filter out stray, confusing background noises and focus on the specific item to be inspected. Basic inspection methods are extremely simple and require very little training. For those who require more sophistication, UE Systems and SDT offer training courses that range from one-day specialized classes to five-day certifiable courses. Reliabilityweb.com Publishing also publishes an excellent ultrasound reference book titled *Hear More* (ISBN 9780982516331), available at Amazon.com or the MRO-Zone.com bookstore.

Ultrasonic condition analysis is straightforward. Users of analog instruments can observe sound levels while simultaneously listening to the sound quality. Digital users have additional options such as sound and data analysis through specialized software. The more sophisticated digital instruments provide features for comprehensive mechanical or bearing condition monitoring programs, including data logging, software for trending and creation of alarm groups, sound sample recording, spectral analysis of sounds, and software with customizable reporting formats.

How Ultrasound Bearing and Mechanical Inspection Works

Mechanical movements produce a wide spectrum of sound. One of the major contributors to excessive stress in machinery is friction. Ultrasound instruments detect friction. By focusing on a narrow band of high frequencies, the instrument detects subtle changes in amplitude and sound quality produced by operating equipment. It then heterodynes these normally undetectable sounds down into the audible range where they are heard through headphones and observed on a display panel for trending, comparison, and analysis.

It has been established that ultrasound monitoring provides early warning of bearing failure. Various stages of bearing failure have been established. An 8 dB gain over baseline indicates pre-failure or lack of lubrication. A 12 dB increase establishes the very beginning of the failure mode. A 16 dB gain indicates advanced failure condition while a 35–50 dB gain warns of catastrophic failure. For those who utilize ultrasound spectral analysis, these conditions can often be observed through both FFT and time series analysis.

Ultrasonic Bearing Inspection Method

There are three methods for ultrasonic bearing monitoring: comparative, historical, and analytical. In order to note possible deviations that might indicate a potential failure condition or to establish a baseline for future surveys, it is necessary to compare similar bearings with one another for potential differences in amplitude and sound quality. To do this, make a permanent reference point on a bearing housing or use the grease fitting, then tune to 30 kHz and adjust the received sound level (in analog instruments this is the "Sensitivity" dial) so that the intensity or decibel level can be observed on the display panel. Then compare this base reading with similar bearings. Once a series of bearings have been tested, and a baseline set, data is recorded and then compared with future readings for historical trending and analysis. Alarm levels can be set to note any bearings in need of corrective action. An 8 dB gain over a baseline with no change in sound quality will indicate possible lubrication starvation. Levels that are 12 dB or higher can signify a potential failed condition. The analytical approach can be integrated into the comparative or historical process. Sound anomalies can be recorded and analyzed through spectral analysis software. Some of the advanced instruments have on-board spectral analysis, providing the ability to diagnose issues while performing inspections out in the plant. (Ref. 4)

Some Misconceptions Regarding Airborne Ultrasound

I would like to close this chapter by addressing a few common misconceptions about airborne ultrasound technology. First is the misconception that, "Our plant is so loud, that thing will not be able distinguish one noisy piece of equipment from the next."

The noise you hear at your plant with your ears is in a completely different range of sound from what you can hear with the equipment. So regardless of how loud your plant is, the instrument will always be effective in detecting failures and faults. As an example, I saw a PdM technician proving to a plant manager and an engineer that he could detect small air leaks from as far away as 30 feet over the roar of steam leaks, pumps, motors, and conveyors in the background.

The second misconception I often address as I perform RCMs is actually an excuse: "Well, we don't have the money to get into the PdM business right now. These fancy tools cost lots of money, and money is hard to come by these days."

To this I offer the following business case: At companies around the world, I ask engineers and managers the rate of return for capital investment at their company. Most reply that capital projects have to show a return on investment within three years. In the 15 years I have been providing RCM training and facilitation services, I have yet to have a customer who purchased an ultrasonic detection instrument where the instrument did not pay for itself—plus the investment of training the users—within the first three *months* of purchase. In fact, I often wish I had become an airborne ultrasound salesman. Selling these instruments is easier than selling ice cream at a park on a hot summer day!

The last misconception I want to cover is in regard to training your people to use the instrument. A common excuse sounds like this: "Well, we would like to get involved in the technology, but we don't have anyone who is trained, and I hear it takes years of experience to become a good PdM technician."

This is where airborne ultrasound differs from every other PdM technology. With just a few hours of training and a quick trip around your plant with a certified instructor, one of your people can be trained to identify, measure, and calculate the loss of air leaks at your facility and in no time at all begin saving the money it took to purchase the best instrument available and the training to use it! It was only a few years ago that I took the training myself, and in the same day I was trained I was able to identify and tag nearly 50 compressed air leaks. The beauty of this technology and the instrument is how easy it is to learn and use.

Reference Notes:

1. Gary Mohr, UE Systems Inc.

2. Pressurized Condensate Return Systems – Kelly Paffel, technical manager, Plant Support & Evaluations Inc.
http://www.plantsupport.com/download/PSE_BP_8.pdf

3. Applying Airborne Ultrasound to Electrical Components
http://www.uesystems.com/applications/electrical-inspection.aspx

4. Applying Airborne Ultrasound to Mechanical Components
http://www.uesystems.com/applications/mechanical-inspection.aspx

Chapter 3

Electric Motor Reliability

The electric motor has become an extremely important and popular piece of equipment. We can trace the origin of the motor back to 1831, when Michael Faraday succeeded in building the first electric motor by demonstrating the fundamental principles of electromagnetism. Both Faraday and Joseph Henry are credited with building the first experimental electric motor. In 1887, Nikola Tesla introduced the Alternate Current (AC) motor, which was much easier to use and has become the most common style in use today. The prevalence of motors since the early 1900s has exploded. Today, the use of motors spans all sectors of life: industrial, commercial, and private. Motors are used in cars and in many household appliances, such as washing machines, dishwashers, HVAC systems, and even old-fashioned ice cream machines. Motors are frequently used in commercial and industrial sectors to power fans, pumps, and air compressors, which account for more than 50% of the total motor-related electricity consumed. It is safe to say that we have become dependent on the use of motors, and their presence is deeply ingrained in our everyday life.

According to the Department of Energy (DOE), more than 40 million electric motors convert electricity into useful work in U.S. manufacturing operations.

According to the Department of Energy (DOE), more than 40 million electric motors convert electricity into useful work in U.S. manufacturing operations. It is estimated that industry spends more than $30 billion (US) annually on electricity dedicated to electric motor–driven systems. Because nearly 70% of all electricity used in industry is consumed by motor systems, it is believed that increases in the energy efficiency of existing motor systems will lead to dramatic nationwide energy savings. *(Ref. 1)*

In 1992, the DOE's Industrial Technologies Program desired to design a program that would promote increased energy efficiency of motor systems and be responsive to industry needs. This program evolved into the Motor Challenge program, which relies extensively on existing market forces to bring program messages to the end-user. Today, more than 3,000 organizations have joined the program as Motor Challenge Partners. When its Motor Challenge program began, the DOE had estimated that industrial motor-system energy use could be reduced by 11–18% if all existing cost-effective technologies and practices for improved efficiency were implemented. If implemented, the goals for the program were expected to result in annual energy savings of 75 to 122 billion kilowatt-hours (kWh) by 2010, which would lower industry costs by $3.6 to $5.8 billion, along with annual reduction of polluting gases from 42 to 46 million metric tons. Starting in 1994–95 with 21 projects, the DOE's effort sought to publicize case histories of successful system efficiency improvements in order to encourage other users to recognize the benefits and act accordingly. The first two completed projects showed savings of 1.5 million kWh annually. Such case histories can be found on DOE's website: http://www1.eere.energy.gov/industry/bestpractices/case_studies.html.

Before we focus on the major areas of concern for the reliable and efficient operation of motors, we should probably touch on some basics of the motor. A motor is a device that creates motion. More specifically, a motor's function is to convert electrical energy into mechanical energy to perform useful work. There are six common characteristics to consider when comparing, choosing, or purchasing motors. These characteristics are enclosure type, insulation class, operating speed, power, efficiency, and service factor. Let's take a quick look at all six of these.

The enclosure type refers to the motor casing. The National Electric Manufacturers Association (NEMA) classifies motors according to environmental protection and methods of cooling. There are 18 categories, but the two most common enclosure types are Open Drip-Proof (ODP) and Totally Enclosed Fan-Cooled (TEFC). ODP motors have ventilation openings constructed so that the operation will not be affected by solid or liquid particles that strike or enter the enclosure at any angle up to 15 degrees downward from vertical. The ODP enclosure type is common in HVAC fans and pumps. TEFC motors operate in severe environments that require a totally enclosed frame while the exterior surfaces are cooled by an external fan on the motor shaft. Because TEFC motors are used in harsher environments, their capital costs are typically higher.

The motor insulation class is a measure of resistance of the insulating components of a motor to degradation from heat. There are four major classifications of insulation used in motors. They are, in order of increasing thermal capabilities, A, B, F, and H.

Class of Insulation System	Temperature, Degrees Celsius
A	105
B	130
F	155
H	180

Every motor is designed with a specific synchronous speed. This speed represents the speed at which the magnetic field within the motor rotates. It is also the approximate speed the motor will run under no-load conditions. As an example, a 4-pole motor running in 60 cycles would have a magnetic field speed of 1,800 revolutions per minute (RPM). The no-load speed of that motor shaft would be very close to 1,800, probably 1,798 RPM. More than half of motors are 1,800 RPM. Motors of 1,200 and 3,600 RPM also are fairly common. The full-load speed of the same 4-pole motor above might be 1,745 RPM. The difference between the synchronous speed and the full-load speed is called the slip RPM of the motor. It is important to note that efficient motors tend to operate at a slightly higher full-load speed than standard motors do (usually by about 5–10 RPM for 1,800 RPM motors).

The power of a motor represents its capacity to perform a physical task. This power is commonly measured in horsepower (hp) and kilowatts (kW). The horsepower used for electrical motors is defined as exactly 746 Watts, or 1 hp is equivalent to 0.746 kW.

Efficiency is the percentage of the input power that is actually converted to work output from the motor shaft. Nominal efficiency, stamped on the nameplate of most motors, is an average value obtained through standardized testing of a given motor model population running at full capacity.

Efficiency = (746 * hp output) / Watts input

Electric motors are efficient at converting electric energy into mechanical energy. If the efficiency of an electric motor is 90%, it means that 90% of the electrical energy is directly converted to mechanical energy at the motor shaft. The portion lost within the motor is the difference between electrical energy input and mechanical energy output. Efficient use of the electrical energy enables commercial and industrial facilities to minimize operating costs and increase profits to stay competitive.

The motor's service factor represents the allowable overload at which a motor can be run continuously at nameplate voltage and frequency. A service factor of 1.0 indicates that prolonged operation above full load can damage the motor. A service factor of 1.15 is typical for motors 1 hp and above and indicates that the motor can work at 1.15 times its rated horsepower without failing.

As mentioned above, a motor's function is to convert electrical energy to mechanical energy to perform some form of useful work. There is really only one way to improve motor efficiency, and that is to reduce motor losses. Even though standard motors operate efficiently, with typical efficiencies ranging between 83–92%, energy-efficient motors perform significantly better. A slight efficiency gain to 92–94% results in a 25% reduction in losses. (Ref. 2)

Since motor losses result in heat injected into the atmosphere, reducing losses can significantly decrease cooling loads on an industrial facility's air conditioning system. Motor energy losses can be categorized into five major areas, each of which is influenced by design and construction decisions. (Ref. 3) One design consideration is the size of the air gap between the rotor and the stator. Large air gaps tend to maximize efficiency at the expense of power factor, while small air gaps slightly compromise efficiency but significantly improve power factor. (Ref. 4) Motor losses should be categorized as those that are fixed and remain constant for a given voltage and speed, and those that are variable and increase with motor load. (Ref. 5) These losses are described below.

1. **Core loss** represents the energy required to magnetize the core material (hysteresis) and includes losses due to the creation of eddy currents that flow in the core. Core losses can be decreased through the use of improved permeability electromagnetic (silicon) steel and by lengthening the core to reduce magnetic flux densities. Eddy current losses can be decreased by using thinner steel laminations.

2. **Windage and friction losses** occur because of bearing friction, caused by drag during rotation, and air resistance during motor cooling. Improved bearing selection, air flow, and fan design are employed to reduce these losses. In an energy-efficient motor, loss minimization results in reduced cooling requirements, so a smaller fan can be used.

Both core losses and windage and friction losses are independent of motor load.

3. **Stator losses** are the largest losses in a motor and appear as heating occurs because current is flowing (I) through the resistance (R) of the stator winding. This is commonly referred to as an I2R loss. I2R losses can be decreased by modifying the stator slot design or by decreasing insulation thickness to increase the volume of wire in the stator.

4. **Rotor losses** appear as I2R heating in the rotor winding. Rotor losses can be reduced by increasing the size of the conductive bars and end rings to produce a lower resistance, or by reducing the electrical current.

5. **Stray load losses** are the result of leakage fluxes induced by load currents. Both stray load losses and stator and rotor I2R losses increase with motor load.

Motor loss components are summarized in the table below. *(Ref. 6)*

Motor Loss Categories

No Load Losses	Typical Losses (%)	Factors Affecting these Losses
Core Losses	15 - 25%	Type and quantity of magnetic material
Friction and Windage Losses	5 - 15%	Selection and design of fans and bearings
Motor Operating Under Load		
Stator I2R Losses	25 - 40%	Stator conductor size
Rotor I2R Losses	15 - 25%	Rotor conductor size
Stray Load Losses	10 - 20%	Manufacturing and design methods

It's important to note that while the losses are categorized above into no load and operating under load, all these losses can be effectively addressed during the design phase of a project. While most of them can be identified using a predictive technology such as Infrared Thermography or Motor Current Signature Analysis, to eliminate the root cause of the defect will require a system redesign or in some come cases component replacement. Reliability in its truest form starts with engineering and design, and it should not be overlooked or the first thing to be removed in order to save costs, because shortcuts in this phase add exponentially to the life cycle cost of the system.

In 1997, the Energy Policy Act (EPACT) required all motors sold in the United States to meet efficiency standards. In 2001, a new class of premium efficiency motors was designated, setting efficiency standards for new motors beyond those of EPACT. Motors labeled as "NEMA Premium" are about 1–7% more efficient than standard-efficiency motors. Since operating costs comprise the majority of lifetime equipment costs, even a 1% gain in efficiency can make a big difference. The higher purchase price for premium efficiency motors is recouped through lower electricity bills. NEMA Premium motors also run cooler and are more likely to better withstand voltage variations and harmonics.

Annual Energy Cost Savings with 1,800 RPM NEMA Premium-Efficiency ODP Motors Rated 600 Volts or Less

HP	RPM	Standard Efficiency (Source: Motor Master)	NEMA Premium Efficiency (Source: www.nema.org)	kW Reduction	Annual Energy Cost Savings
1	1800	76.50%	85.50%	0.07	$ 19.39
1.5	1800	77.40%	86.50%	0.10	$ 29.40
2	1800	79.70%	86.50%	0.10	$ 29.30
3	1800	82.60%	89.50%	0.15	$ 44.59
5	1800	84.10%	89.50%	0.20	$ 58.16
7.5	1800	85.90%	91.00%	0.29	$ 82.39
10	1800	86.90%	91.70%	0.36	$ 103.40

Most energy-efficient motors utilize some of the following techniques to reduce or minimize losses:

- Use of wire with lower resistance

- Improved design of the rotor electric circuit

- Higher permeability in the magnetic circuits of the stator and rotor

- Use of thinner steel laminations in the magnetic circuits

- Improved shape of the steel stator core and rotor magnetic circuits

- Smaller gap between stator and rotor

- Internal fan, cooling fins, and cooling air passages designed to reduce the cooling power requirement

- Use of bearings with lower friction

Beginning in December 2010 the new Energy Independence and Security Act of 2007 (EISA) government regulations changed motor manufacturers' requirements for meeting NEMA Premium standards for NEMA and IEC frame sizes on motors less than 600 volts. A few of the items that were implemented include:

The following motor categories, not previously required to meet EPACT efficiency levels, are now required: 8-pole motors, close coupled pump motors, Design C, U-frame motors, 3-phase motors of not more than 600 volts (other than 230V or 460V) including IEC frame motors from 90 frame and up, C-face or D-flange without base. In addition, 201–500 hp motors not previously covered by EPACT will be required to comply with energy efficiencies as defined by NEMA MG 1 Table 12-11, Vertical solid shaft normal thrust motors (p-base) as tested in a horizontal configuration.

The following motor categories must meet NEMA Premium: 200 hp and below general purpose, Polyphase design A and B up to 600VAC, TEFC, ODP, explosion proof, brake motors, NEMA 140T frames to 449, foot mounted, C-face foot mounted, severe duty, washdown, etc., IEC Metric 90 frames and larger.

Although manufacturers were given a two-year extension for compliance in the original EPACT regulation, the EISA regulation required all hazardous location motors to move to NEMA Premium standards in December 2010.

This new Energy Independence and Security Act of 2007 (EISA) was recently summarized in a series of emails by PdMA Corporation to highlight some of the issues that may impact many end-users. *(Ref. 7)*

Although high-efficiency motors have been available for years, they make up less than 10% of all industrial motors in current use. If your motors are not part of this 10%, they could be using excess electricity, decreasing reliability and increasing your operating costs. With that being said, since the improvement achievable in efficiency is only a small percentage, it is normally not economically viable to replace an existing motor with a premium efficiency motor merely based on possible savings. However, in the case of new installations or motor replacements, premium efficiency motors should be considered over standard ones as the savings normally pay for the incremental cost of the higher efficiency motors. The operating cost of a typical motor far exceeds the initial capital expense. A heavily used motor may cost up to 10 times the purchase price to operate per year. When you buy a motor, choose the most energy-efficient and affordable model. Premium efficiency motors cost about 20% more but will pay back in less than four years with one-shift operation and a cost of 5 cents per kWh. Payback will be shorter for a 24-hour, seven-day-per-week operation. Savings can be estimated for each case by using the following formula:

$$Energy\ Saved\ in\ kWh = motor\ kW\ \times Operating\ hours\ \times\ \left[\frac{1}{ns} - \frac{1}{np}\right]$$

$$where\ ns = efficiency\ of\ standard\ motor, and\ np = efficiency\ of\ premium\ motor$$

Let's take a look at some basic strategies for reducing motor electricity use. Since motors operate as one component of a larger asset and system, it is critical to evaluate the related impacts of any change before deciding which approaches to take. Now, I realize that many of these strategies seem either too basic or too easy, but I have been in numerous facilities all over the world and continue to find that many of these simple techniques are often overlooked and not implemented. Before we can address reliable operation and the technologies we can utilize to ensure such operation, we have to evaluate the basic approach and any behavioral changes required.

Are your motors running when they are not needed? I walked into a plant one day and noticed an entire line running as if it was running production. When I asked the simple question about whether they were warming up for production, I was told the line had not been running production for the past three days and was not scheduled to run production for another three days. When inquiring about the reason for not shutting down the equipment, I was told things just never seem to start up without problems, so they run the entire line regardless. This type of behavior increases energy costs and equipment wear. I understand that unnecessary starts/stops of motors, especially larger ones, is not good and actually has the potential to create coil movement, which could result in shorted windings, but in this particular case the reasoning does not hold true. If you are able, you should look for opportunities to turn things off. It is similar to my parents always telling me as a child to turn my bedroom lights off when I was not in my bedroom. Can you turn off motors for hot water circulation, air compressors, or ventilation fans at night (assuming you don't run all three shifts)? In some situations, it is appropriate to switch off the motor manually. For most applications, you can make the task easier by installing timers or sensors to switch the motor on and off.

Energy use can be significantly cut simply by reducing the speed of an HVAC fan. The energy consumption of fans and pumps varies according to the speed raised to the third power, so small changes in speed can make big changes in energy consumption. For example, power consumption can almost be cut in half by using a 5 hp motor versus a 10 hp motor, with both of them being rated at 1,780 RPM full-load speed. HVAC equipment can often be reset on-site by an HVAC technician if a slower speed will still deliver the necessary airflow. But before doing so, ensure that reducing fan speeds won't adversely affect indoor conditions. Most air conditioning equipment is designed to deliver about 400 cubic feet per minute of airflow per ton of cooling capacity in order to function properly.

Many motors operate at a constant speed all the time, regardless of need. A variable frequency drive (VFD) matches the motor's speed to the load, allowing the motor to be continually adjusted relative to the power needed. A VFD can cut energy use and reduce wear and tear on the motor and its related components. A 20% reduction in fan speed, for example, can reduce energy consumption by nearly 50%. Good applications for VFDs include large motors that can operate for several hours at reduced speed and motors with loads that vary from day to night or seasonally. Another advantage of VFDs is that they are often equipped with soft starting features that decrease motor starting current to about 1.5 to 2 times the operating current. VFDs can dramatically reduce the impact of fan starts on an electrical system. VFDs also reduce the voltage sag that can occur when a large motor starts quickly. Voltage sags can dim lights and cause other equipment to shut down or restart. Consider using a VFD motor system instead of traditional motors when your loads vary significantly over the course of daily use.

You may be able to reduce the load on a motor and save energy by reducing pressure losses in pipe and duct runs with low-pressure loss elbows and fittings. Duct and pipe systems with lower pressure losses can often use a slower speed fan or pump to deliver the same amount of flow. This simple technique can result in big savings. Other ways to reduce the load on a motor system include aligning the motor drive and replacing inefficient drivetrains such as belts, chains, and gears with direct drive systems.

As mentioned in our chapter regarding electrical power distribution, addressing any power quality problems will ensure not only equipment reliability but will also affect electrical efficiency. To improve motor reliability and efficiency, it is important to maintain the correct voltage and phase balance, identify and eliminate current leaks, and prevent harmonics in the electrical supply. When the line voltages applied to a polyphase induction motor are not equal, unbalanced currents in the stator windings occur. A small percentage of voltage unbalance results in a much larger percentage of current unbalance. Consequently, the temperature rise of the motor operating at a particular load and percentage voltage unbalance will be greater than that of a motor operating under the same conditions with balance voltages. Keep in mind, heat reduces a motor's useful life and adversely affects supply feeder components. A 2% voltage imbalance can increase motor loss by as much as 10%, raise motor winding temperature by 8°C and decrease efficiency by 1%. According to the Electrical Apparatus Service Association (EASA), a 10°C temperature rise halves motor winding life expectancy.

Unbalanced currents and reverse rotation from voltage imbalance produce energy waste and reduced motor efficiency. The reduction in motor efficiency is proportional to the imbalance and is more pronounced at reduced motor load (as shown in table below).

Motor Efficiency Loss from Voltage Imbalance at Reduced Load *(Ref. 8)*

% Motor Load	Balanced	1% Imbalance	2.5% Imbalance
100	0.00%	0.00%	1.50%
75	0.00%	0.10%	1.40%
50	0.00%	0.60%	2.10%

It is a good idea to have an electrical engineer review the electrical system periodically, especially before installing a new motor or after making changes to the system and its loads. The voltage at the motor should be as close to the design limits, found on the nameplate, as possible. Changes of more than 5% can lead to a 2–4% drop in efficiency and increased temperatures, which decrease the motor's life. Voltage at the motor that is not within the design limits leads to a decrease in power factor. Low power factors may be penalized by your power company. A tremendous opportunity many of us have is to incorporate continuous power monitoring into our maintenance strategy. Continuous monitoring has the potential to reveal the condition of the entire manufacturing process. When defects or events occur within the electrical and/or mechanical equipment, we will certainly see an impact, positive or negative, on energy consumption.

Have you ever witnessed an oversized motor? Motors are oversized when the power end requirements are less than the motor is capable of producing. For example, when a 10 hp motor is used for an application that calls for a 5 hp motor, the motor is 100% oversized, or operates at 50% full load. Why do people oversize motors when designing a system? I used to work for an electrical engineer who had a rule of thumb to oversize all motors, regardless of application, by 50%, with the logic of ensuring for future demand should expansion of the system and/or production requirements occur. I often wondered how much sense this made. An oversized motor will run at lower efficiencies, which result in increased energy costs. Not only that, but the purchase price is more. The efficiency of most motors peaks at around 75–80% of full load and drops off sharply below 40–50% of full load, although these ranges vary by design and manufacturer. To optimize efficiency, a motor should be sized to operate with a load factor of 60–75%. At smaller load factors motor efficiency is lower, leading to higher operating costs. Select a lower power motor and operate it at a higher load factor to help justify the motor replacement. Motors operated at low load factors have lower power factors. Motors loaded below 50% may be attractive candidates for replacement. Since the relationship between efficiency and load varies among different types and sizes of motors, be sure to check with the manufacturer or building engineer before replacing an oversized motor.

Proper maintenance goes a long way toward improving the efficiency and equipment life. For maximum performance and greatest energy efficiency, one should perform basic preventive maintenance tasks, such as lubrication of drivetrains (bearings, chains, and gears), proper drive belt tension, cleaning fan blades, replacing air filters regularly, and cleaning motor cooling fins and keeping them free from debris. Motors should have good ventilation and be periodically inspected for increased vibration or power supply problems. The right maintenance actions at the right time pay for themselves with longer-lasting equipment and less downtime; energy savings shorten the payback even further.

Safeguard against thermal damage by avoiding conditions that contribute to overheating. These include dirt, under- and over-voltage, voltage imbalance, harmonics, high ambient temperature, poor ventilation, and overload operation (even within the service factor).

A few years ago, on a Thursday afternoon, workers at an industrial facility found themselves looking at a motor in the final stages of failure. The maintenance department determined that this motor was beyond simple repair and would cost approximately $90,000 to completely rebuild. The immediate problem was that this motor was critical to a portion of the process, and losing the motor would result in losing an entire production run—a

$400,000 implication. The motor needed to run until Sunday afternoon, just four more days. Have you ever been in a similar predicament? What did you do? Well, this plant decided that there was only one option: They took the chance and ran the motor, hoping it would last until the end of the production cycle. Can you guess the outcome? Murphy's Law came into effect ("Anything that can go wrong will go wrong"), and the motor didn't make it. The plant lost $490,000. We always ask our clients about scenarios like this. From a maintenance and reliability standpoint, there are four questions that needed to be answered to learn from this situation:

1. How long have we known about the defect that caused this problem?

2. How many opportunities have we had to deal with this issue since we learned about it?

3. How much would it have cost us to deal with this immediately upon learning about it?

4. What changes to our processes and procedures do we need to make to ensure we never again find ourselves in this position again?

We believe that these four questions should be asked and answered every single time there is an emergency repair, a breakdown, a schedule breaker, or a high-priority job. We do this to fuel the continuous improvement process.

So, you might be wondering for the case above what the answers to these questions were, and I will share those with you in order. The plant supervisors had been notified through a routine infrared thermography route of the defect that caused the motor problem for six months leading up to the catastrophic failure. The plant had experienced two scheduled shutdowns during the previous six months and could have addressed the issue if it had been a priority. If they had addressed the problem immediately upon learning about it, it would have cost them less than one hour of labor for one person and at most a few hours of engineering for long-term root cause elimination. Hard to believe until you find out that the problem was an overheated motor due to product overflow plugging the cooling fins of the motor. And the answer to the last question leads to many solutions addressing planning, scheduling, culture, and behavioral changes. Just because we utilize technology and other means of maintenance doesn't mean that we will save money or run reliably. We must have the culture built to improve along with the processes and procedures in place to drive the behavior we expect and the results we want.

24

Consider a similar defect shown below on a primary centrifuge motor. The fan cover on the motor was discovered to be completely restricted. The fan cover was cleaned, and new images were taken 12 minutes later. The results show a significant drop in temperatures over the entire motor. The first two IR images were taken on the south side of the motor; they show that there is an average temperature drop of 24°F. The second group of IR images was taken on the north side of the motor; they show a temperature drop of 15°F. The final two pictures are digital images of the fan cover before and after cleaning.

Image shows as-found condition of the motor.

Image shows condition of the motor after being cleaned.

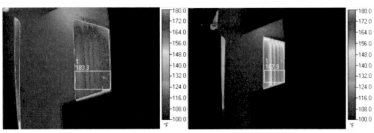

Image shows as-found condition of the motor.

Image shows condition of the motor after being cleaned.

Image shows fan cover almost completely restricted.

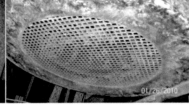

Image shows fan cover after being cleaned.

Bearing failures account for nearly half of all motor failures. If not detected in time, the failing bearing can cause overheating and damage insulation, or it can fail drastically and do irreparable mechanical damage to the motor. Vibration trending is an excellent way to detect bearing problems in time to intervene.

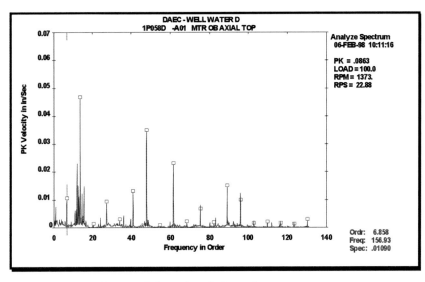

Bearing defects identified on vibration spectrum.

Given the movement and effort to go green, maintenance management may overlook the fact that maintaining reliability can pay dividends toward efficiency while improving the bottom line. The ideal approach would use technologies to provide data that would help companies make the right choice between repairing or replacing motors that are pushing the environmentally friendly envelope of efficiency and be used to maintain and improve motor reliability. We will discuss this in a bit more detail in the last chapter, "Reliability and Energy, the Allied Way."

In regard to motors, one such technology is the PdMA Corporation MCEmax motor test equipment powered by MCEGold software. This technology combination provides the ability for a complete electrical analysis of six crucial areas of motor function known as electric motor fault zones. Not only will the analysis of these six fault zones provide a deep understanding of the motor's health, but it will also allow energy analysis to assist in making educated decisions toward repairing or replacing motors. The six fault zones are:

1. Power Quality. The focus on this fault zone follows the increasing use and reliance on AC and DC drives. An ongoing concern about the power quality is the possibility of distortion of voltage and current levels from variable frequency drives. Some sources of trouble with power quality include non-linear loads, starting and stopping of nearby equipment, and voltage spikes. These types of power phenomena influences can cause excessive harmonics on the distribution system, which can result in overheating of the insulation system. The presence of harmonics in a distribution system produces excessive heat because of increasing current demands. If this is left undetected, heat above acceptable levels can either lead to motor malfunctions or shorten the motor's life.

2. Power Circuit. This fault zone is defined as the system of conductors and connections running from the point of origin of testing to the connections at the motor. The circuit can include breakers, fuses, contactors, and lug connections. There should be no doubt that a problem in the power circuit impairs efficiency. A study conducted in the mid-1990s determined that more than 46% of the faults found in industrial power distribution systems that reduced motor efficiency stemmed from difficulties within either the connectors or conductors. These types of difficulties lead to high-resistance connections in the power circuit, which cause unbalanced terminal voltages at the motor. As we discussed earlier, unbalanced terminal voltages result in overheating of components, loss of torque, overheating of the motor

insulation system, and a decrease in motor efficiency. Faulty power circuit conditions place the most efficient and well-maintained motors at risk for reduced horsepower that can lead to excessive heat and insulation damage.

3. Insulation. There is potential for damage to the insulation between the windings and the ground, which is generally caused by contamination, high temperatures, and moisture. A faulty power circuit is generally the culprit in insulation damage, but advanced testing is required to determine whether the damage was caused by motor disruption or another problem yet to be analyzed.

4. Stator. A stator consists of copper windings connected with solder joints between the coils. Outside of design or manufacturing defects, the stator is often the symptom of another fault mechanism. The goal for stator-related incidents is to identify conditions conducive to stator defects and correct them before they cause a stator failure. Stator failures can often be catastrophic, resulting in unplanned outages and defective products, which increase the use of energy and create waste.

5. Rotor. In more specific terms, the rotor fault zone refers to the rotor bars, laminations, and end rings. The percentage of motor failures attributed to rotor problems is low, but their trouble spots can cause extensive damage to the motor if left unchecked. Because of its close proximity to the rotor, the stator is also at risk. For example, a cracked rotor bar will lead to heat buildup intense enough to melt insulation on its laminations as well as on the nearby stator. This is another case where motor efficiency will be compromised without the advanced technology necessary to detect cracked or broken rotor bars.

6. Air Gap. The gap between the rotor and stator assures efficiency when it is evenly distributed around 360 degrees of the motor. When air gap distribution is uneven or non-symmetric, the usual result is an unbalanced magnetic field and high vibration levels. If undetected, over time these elevated levels of vibration can result in excessive movement of the stator winding, which could lead to increased friction and eventually turn-to-turn, coil-to-coil, or ground faults. Additionally, the vibration can accelerate bearing failure, which could seize the shaft of the motor and overheat the windings or allow additional movement of the shaft, which could lead to a rotor stator rub. If these events occur and are not addressed properly, mechanical looseness could develop in

the rotor. Any of these occurrences could lead to a catastrophic failure of the motor, which could require a complete rewind and possible restacking of the iron. Whether brought about by bearing failure or a rotor stator rub, these increased losses have a direct impact on the operating efficiency of the motor.

All six of these fault zones require ongoing testing of the highest standards and tolerances to effectively assure efficiency and reliability. As with the studies that show the correlation between safety and reliability, when it comes to efficiency and reliability, it is highly unlikely that you will achieve one without the other. Being clean or going green without keeping all three of these items (safety, reliability, and efficiency) in mind is an impossible task. (*Ref. 9*)

Reference Notes:

1. Paul E. Scheihing, "U.S. Department of Energy's Motor Challenge Program: A National Strategy for Energy Efficient Industrial Motor-Driven Systems," Department of Energy Industrial Technologies Program, http://www1.eere.energy.gov/industry/bestpractices/motor_challenge_national_strategy.html.

2. Gilbert A. McCoy, Todd Litman, and John G. Douglass, "Energy-Efficient Electric Motor Selection Handbook" (Revision 3), Washington State Energy Office, January 1993.

3. John R. Keinz and R.L. Hotulton, "NEMA/Nominal Efficiency: What Is It and Why?" IEEE Conference Record, CH1459-5, Paper No. PCI-80-8, 1980.

4. Austin H. Bonnett, "Understanding Efficiency and Power Factor in Squirrel Cage Induction Motors," U.S. Electrical Motors, Presentation to the Washington State Energy Office, April 1990.

5. David C. Montgomery, "How to Specify and Evaluate Energy-Efficient Motors," General Electric Company.

6. Gilbert A. McCoy, Todd Litman, and John G. Douglass, "Energy-Efficient Electric Motor Selection Handbook" (Revision 3), Washington State Energy Office, January 1993.

7. PdMA Corporation, *Electrical Motor Testing Tips*. www.pdma.com.

8. Doty S., *Commercial Energy Auditing Reference Handbook*, Fairmont Press, 2008.

9. Noah Bethel, "Motor Efficiency and Fault Zone Analysis," PdMA Corporation.

Chapter 4

Air Handling Systems Reliability

erhaps the most commonly used asset around the world, Heating, Ventilating, and Air Conditioning (HVAC) systems are in most cases ripe for a few changes in design and maintenance practices that will have a direct impact on their reliability and energy efficiency. As a general rule, HVAC systems are installed, balanced on start-up, and then promptly ignored. Over time we make what we view as minor changes to the system based on the ever-changing location of office space and peoples' personal sense of it being too hot or too cold to work. We gradually collect small space heaters and fans to help compensate for individual preferences, and in many cases the maintenance people will install dummy thermostats in hopes that as each office person makes an adjustment up or down, the act of making a change will have a placebo effect, thus saving them from having to actually make changes.

As a general rule, HVAC systems are installed, balanced on start-up, and then promptly ignored.

The Department of Energy estimates that up to 35% of power used at manufacturing facilities is for HVAC. Do you have a sound maintenance strategy for keeping your HVAC systems energy efficient and reliable?

In 15 years I have never performed an RCM analysis on an HVAC system. Unless we are talking about a clean room environment, the HVAC system typically doesn't rank too high when it comes to asset criticality ranking. Because of this, we are now looking at a system that will be ignored in terms of routine maintenance. Like any other asset made up of mechanical and electrical components, if it is ignored long enough the efficiency will degrade over time and ultimately cause system shutdown. But does that mean run to failure is the most cost-efficient maintenance strategy? Could improving the reliability and energy efficiency of these assets result in a return on investment for taking the time to properly balance and maintain the system? Let's take a look. (*Interesting… Months after I wrote this chapter, I facilitated my first RCM on an HVAC system. The system was highly critical as it serviced a clean room environment for a pharmaceutical company.*)

When I first began to research energy-efficiency improvements for HVAC systems, I began with the Energy Star Program, a joint effort of the Environmental Protection Agency (EPA) and the Department of Energy (DOE). They have loads of information online, including a 170-page PDF on building upgrades. It seems that the Energy Star answer to energy efficiency is to replace your old, outdated, and inefficient building assets with newer and more energy-efficient products. The document is thorough, starting with how to build a business case for upgrading your lighting, insulation, controls, and HVAC equipment. While there are many pages of valuable information, I wanted to trim it down to a few pages of useful information on how to get the most out of making your building's HVAC system more energy efficient and reliable.

Taking the simple man's approach, let's start with the outside air intake and work our way through the typical system to the point where air is delivered to the work area and returned to be mixed again with outside air. The typical HVAC system begins with an outside air damper that regulates the amount of outside air taken in by the system. This outside air is now mixed with return air and filtered to remove dirt, dust, bugs, or other solid particles. Once the air has been filtered, it enters a centrifugal fan and is pushed through a series of coils where the air is heated or cooled depending on the season and desired work condition temperature. At this point, depending on your location and environment, the air may be humidified or dehumidified and pushed through the ductwork to various locations at your plant. Within the ductwork we will have a number of dampers and registers to balance the airflow to various locations. To keep the air at a regulated temperature we must have a constant flow of air back to air intake; this is accomplished through return air registers or building exhaust, again depending on your work environment. In the manufacturing world we like to view the HVAC system as a simple process, and as a result it receives very little attention until it is not working. To make the system more reliable and energy efficient, let's break it down to its basic functions:

1. **Heating**
2. **Cooling**
3. **Humidifying**
4. **Dehumidifying**
5. **Ventilation**

While we have what looks like five simple systems, there are a number of ways that each can be accomplished, and this is why there are a limited number of companies that offer plans or services for making your specific system more energy efficient. The best place to start when looking to make your system more reliable and energy efficient is by developing a complete maintenance strategy. The best way to develop a complete maintenance strategy is to perform a reliability-centered maintenance analysis—and, of course, I would recommend you use RCM Blitz™ to complete that analysis. While I started this chapter stating that I have never had a company request an RCM analysis on its HVAC system, I would guess that most companies have no idea how much money they spend or waste when it comes to HVAC. When I looked at several sources while writing this chapter, I found that the average company spends up to 35% of its energy on HVAC. (*Ref. 1*)

Using an RCM approach, let's define the main function of your typical HVAC system.

Main Function: **To be able to provide XXX CFM of air at a temperature of 68–70°F, at a humidity of 30–55%, while meeting all health, safety, and environmental standards.**

We should also view the main function with the assumption that we want to provide these standards while we are utilizing the facility. If we are working 24 hours a day for five days a week, then we need to provide this main function all of that time. In order to develop our maintenance strategy we need to know how the main function can fail; in RCM terms this is known as functional failure. Understanding the functional failures will help us to identify potential failure modes and then develop mitigating maintenance tasks to ensure reliability and energy efficiency.

Functional Failures

1. **Unable to supply air at all**
2. **Unable to supply XXX CFM of air**
3. **Unable to supply air at a temperature of 68–70°F**
4. **Unable to supply air at a humidity of 30–55%**
5. **Unable to maintain health, safety, and environmental standards**

The next step of the RCM process would be to discover all the failure modes and effects for the HVAC, starting with the failure modes associated with being unable to supply air at all and working through all the failure modes for each functional failure. The objective of the analysis is to then develop tasks to mitigate each failure mode by:

1. **Eliminating the failure mode**
2. **Detecting the failure mode through the use of condition-based tools**
3. **Reducing the likelihood of failure through preventive maintenance**
4. **Reducing the consequences of the failure with consequence reduction tasks**

The finished product would be a combination of Preventive Maintenance tasks (PMs), Predictive Maintenance tasks (PdM), failure finding tasks, redesigns, and consequence reduction tasks that ensure the reliability of the asset. Without specific knowledge of the context in which we plan to operate the HVAC system I described above, I cannot complete a thorough RCM analysis of this system. In the spirit of offering suggestions to improve reliability and energy efficiency, I would offer the following general suggestions.

HVAC System Operation

1. Optimize your system by having it balanced by a professional at least once each year to ensure that OSHA exchange of air requirements are being maintained.

2. Use a variable speed drive for your HVAC system to improve efficiency.

3. Automate system controls and make sure you have separate controls for separate zones.

4. Determine day- and nighttime settings for the system.

5. Eliminate unnecessary heating and cooling zones.

6. Control who has the ability to change temperature control settings.

7. Allow a fluctuation in temperature, usually in the range of 68–70°F for heating and 78–80° for cooling.

8. Install an economizer cycle. Instead of operating on a fixed minimum airflow supply, an economizer allows the HVAC system to utilize outdoor air by varying the supply airflow according to outdoor air conditions, usually using an outdoor dry bulb temperature sensor or return air enthalpy (enthalpy switchover). Enthalpy switchover is more efficient because it is based on the true heat content of the air.

9. Control all outside air sources (doors and windows).

10. Minimize exhaust and makeup air.

11. Seal ducts that run through unconditioned space. (The DOE estimates that up to 20% of conditioned air is lost through supply air duct leaks.)

12. Clean heating and cooling coils to improve airflow and heat transfer.

13. Use the system only when and where it is needed:

    • Reduce your system requirements in the off-hours.

    • Heat or cool only space that is being occupied (conference rooms).

HVAC Maintenance

1. Replace HEPA filters based on differential pressure instead of time. HEPA filters are expensive enough to begin with, and as they become fouled the amount of energy used to pull the air through the filter increases significantly.

2. Replace lower-cost front-end air filters based on time or condition.

3. Perform an annual PM inspection of the air intake to ensure it is operable. (The specifics of PM will vary depending on the type of damper and control.)

4. Clean heating and cooling coil surfaces twice each year, in the spring and fall (heating coils, cooling coils, heat exchangers, evaporators, and condensers).

5. Inspect ducts for leaks. Open the inspection ports, seal all leaks, and ensure that the inspection doors are closed and sealed.

6. Inspect drive motor belts for evidence of cracking or fraying, and replace if noted.

7. Ensure that the belt drive has been precision aligned at installation and replacement.

8. Clean and balance the fan. Ensure that your fan has been precision balanced when it is installed, then inspect the fan for cleanliness every year. If you do a sufficient job of replacing filters, there should be no buildup on this fan.

9. Calibrate thermostats and control loops on an annual basis.

10. Maintain steam traps utilizing ultrasonic leak detection methods as well as infrared (IR) inspection on a monthly and quarterly basis in the heating season.

11. Ensure heating and cooling is controlled to +/- 2°F.

12. Test refrigerant lines for leaks, and repair if noted. (Calculate the efficiency of your chillers and check to see if a more energy-efficient unit can be installed.)

Reference Notes:

1. N.C. Division of Pollution Prevention and Environmental Assistance, "Energy Efficiency in Industrial HVAC Systems," September 2003, http://www.p2pays.org/ref/26/25985.pdf.

Chapter 5

Air/Gas Conveyance Systems

Thousands of companies around the world use positive (push) or negative (vacuum) pneumatic conveyance systems to move materials such as grains, powders, and pellets from point A to point B. Some of the advantages of pneumatic conveyors are:

- They are self-cleaning. When we finish conveying the product, the airflow cleans the system of residual product.

- They typically are safer than using an auger or screw conveyor.

- They create less dust at the intake side of the system.

- They cause less breakdown of product than mechanical conveyors.

When it comes to pneumatic conveyors, energy efficiency starts with the fan or blower itself.

Meanwhile, one of the more significant downsides of pneumatic conveyors is the amount of power required for the capacity moved. (*Ref. 1*)

While I have seen more than a couple hundred applications of pneumatic conveyors in my capacity as a maintenance mechanic and reliability engineer, I could count on one hand the number of these conveyors that were designed, maintained, and operated in an efficient manner.

When it comes to pneumatic conveyors, energy efficiency starts with the fan or blower itself. Fan selection is a complex process that starts with a basic knowledge of system operating requirements as well as knowledge of conditions such as airflow rates, temperatures, pressures, airstream properties, and system layout. Other considerations include cost (do we plan to buy the most reliable fan or the lowest-cost fan?), efficiency, operating life, maintenance, speed, material type, space constraints, drive arrangements (direct drive, V-belt, cog belt), temperature, and range of operating conditions.

Although many companies tend to rely on suppliers to make recommendations regarding fan selection, I would recommend they engineer the system for reliability and energy efficiency from concept to installation. Fan performance is typically defined by a plot of developed pressure and power required over a range of fan-generated airflow. Understanding this relationship is essential to designing, sourcing, and operating a fan system and is the key to optimum fan selection.

The reliability of the fan itself begins with the design of the system. It is critical that we take into consideration both the fan efficiency curve and its best efficiency point (BEP), where a fan operates most cost-effectively in terms of both energy efficiency and maintenance considerations. Operating a fan near its BEP improves its performance and reduces wear, allowing longer intervals between repairs. Moving a fan's operating point away from its BEP increases bearing loads, noise, and energy efficiency. (*Ref. 2*)

With the fan properly engineered and sized for the conveyance system, we can now focus on the components that must work with the fan to ensure system balance, efficiency, and reliability. The piping, rotary air valves, cyclone separators, and dust collectors can all have a direct impact on not only the reliability of the system but also the reliability of the fan itself. Should you have a pneumatic conveyance system operating at your plant that is suffering with performance/reliability issues, I would strongly recommend a quick review of the designed performance expectations versus the present operating conditions by collecting data about where your fan is operating within its efficiency curve.

Using this as a starting point, determine which of the following is true:

1. The fan is properly sized, therefore system issues must be causing reliability issues. (Look to determine system component issues that are causing the fan to operate outside of the efficiency curve.)

2. The fan was not properly sized for system requirements, so reliability issues are likely a direct result of the fan operating outside its efficiency curve. (Address fan issues; do not change other system components.)

Common Pneumatic Conveyor System Problems

Understanding how each of the components of your system functions in relationship to your fan is critical in maintaining the reliability and efficiency of your system. A great place to learn proper operation design and new technologies regarding pneumatic conveyance systems is the International Powder and Bulk Solids Conference, which is held in Chicago each year. (*Ref. 3*)

Here is a list of common pneumatic conveyance system problems and good maintenance practices:

1. **Belt Drives:** There are several issues that result from V-belts. Belt wear over time results in slippage, increased vibration, reduced fan output, and secondary damage to the fan and drive motor bearings. It is highly critical that the fan and motor sheaves are precision aligned and that the drive belts are properly tensioned. (Over-tension of the belts results in increased load on the bearings and high bearing vibration.) Product contamination of the belt will also result in increased vibration and premature failure of the fan and motor bearings.

    Precision alignment is the starting point here and should be your primary focus to ensure reliability. Once we have ensured precision alignment, I would strongly recommend a combination of vibration analysis to monitor for any potential failure modes and periodic inspections of the V-belts and sheaves (inspect the belt condition, measure sheave wear, and verify belt tension). I have not recommended an interval here because the operating environment can dictate inspection frequency.

2. **Bearings:** The two biggest issues with the fan and motor bearings come from misalignment and lubrication. If we again ensure precision alignment techniques, we can greatly reduce the likelihood of failure. While lubrication is often perceived as a simple task, companies rarely take the time to ensure that the people who perform lubrication tasks understand the criticality of the task, and this often leads to issues of over-lubrication, under-lubrication, the selection of incorrect lubricants, and contamination of lubricants. The other issue that seems to be growing with the need to reduce costs is installing inferior or low-cost bearings.

The best maintenance practices with fan and motor bearings begin with precision alignment at installation. This should be followed up with monthly vibration analysis and a lubrication task based on bearing type and operating environment that includes: the correct type, amount, and interval. The bearings for this critical system should be identified in your CMMS to ensure that if the bearings fail, they are replaced with the identical bearings (assuming that the bearings identified in the design phase are correct for the application).

3. **Drive Motor:** I hate to sound like a broken record, but we again start with precision alignment. If you want your motors to last, verify that precision alignment is embedded in your maintenance culture. Depending on the location and environment of your equipment, your drive motor should be kept clean and have plenty of airflow for cooling purposes. Allowing this motor to become dirty or having restricted airflow (because of noise issues, it is not uncommon to see these units enclosed in housings) will have a detrimental effect on the life of the motor. Excessive stops and starts can also be very harmful for these units; this most often occurs when the system becomes plugged and operators are trying to clear the plugged section of conveyor piping. Excessive stops and starts result in expansion and embrittlement of the motor windings, which will cause premature motor failures.

Sound maintenance practices for you system motors should include on- and off-line motor current analysis on a quarterly and semiannual basis, monthly vibration analysis of the motor bearings, and quarterly IR inspections of the motor. Motor bearings should be handled in the same manner as the fan bearings. Regularly clean the motor of dirt or dust using a wire brush if your unit is in a dirty environment. (If we keep our systems leak-free and contain our dust, this should not be an issue!) Excessive stops and starts should be addressed through education and training of operators and electricians. Your fan system was not designed to clear plugged conveyance lines; attempting to clear the lines by stopping and starting the conveyor is not only harmful to the motor but also impacts the drive belts and fan itself. Save yourself some time and money and invest in identifying the causes of plugged lines—and eliminate those failures.

4. **Conveyor Piping:** Often the most overlooked and abused part of a pneumatic conveyance system, piping is often the starting point when good systems go bad. The top four issues with conveyance piping are

erosion, improper support, gasket leaks, and physical abuse/damage. Looking at the conveyance piping as it relates to the reliability and efficiency of the conveyance system, we've found that the key is to prevent air, leaks, product leaks, and restrictions. All leaks in the system should be viewed as critical losses. While these leaks may not immediately impact the performance of the system, they do impact the efficiency. Although the system will continue to operate and convey product, the amount of air leaking will directly affect the amount of product the system can move. As we look at the four most common failures of the piping, we see that erosion is the cause that is rarely noticed until the walls wear through. Improper support is also an issue that is often ignored and comes to light through mechanical coupling failures and cracking of welds at flanged connections. If you have ever experienced a conveyance connection failure while the system is in operation (this is not pretty), chances are improper support might be the cause. In terms of gasket failures, being a former pipe fitter I have some strong opinions here. The vast majority of gasket failures come from improper installation (incorrect gasket material and/or fasteners, and improper torque). The most common failure of conveyance piping is physical damage and abuse. This is typically a very bright indication that your system is in trouble, because this abuse and damage is caused by plant personnel hitting the piping with hammers as they attempt to unplug the system. This damage results in two severe effects: piping restrictions and leaks.

Recommended maintenance practices are quite simple if we apply them early in the life of the system. These include the performance of operator rounds inspecting the system for leaks on a daily basis. If a leak has been reported, it should be scheduled for repair as soon as possible. Ensure uniform thickness testing of conveyor piping at 90-degree bends. This will allow us to determine the rate of erosion so we can plan and schedule replacements as needed. Perform annual inspection of piping supports by maintenance while the system is started and operating, and provide training/education about proper gasket materials and torque specifications. Looking at the piping system from a PdM standpoint, I would also recommend continuous monitoring and trend alarms of system airflow and pressure using differential pressure across the fan, dust collector, and cyclone separator. Closing out our plan, we need to ensure that our people understand that they should never hit the piping in an attempt to clear a plug. Not only does this damage the piping but in most cases striking the pipe actually packs the plug tighter. There are several methods and tools for clearing plugged conveyance piping. Learn the correct methods and, most important, determine why the system became plugged and eliminate the cause.

5. **Rotary Air Valves:** These may be the most misunderstood component in a conveyance system. There are four major issues concerning rotary air valves. The first and most common issue is improper installation of the valve. While there are three ways to install a rotary air valve, only one of them is correct, and unless you have had some training or read the OEM, the correct orientation is not immediately evident. If the valve is not properly installed, it will have a direct impact on the efficiency and operation of your system. The second issue is clearance between the valve vanes and end plates and between the vanes and feed throat. As the vanes, end plates, and throat wear, the clearance increases and air will pass through the valve, resulting in air loss, reduced product feed, plugging, and bridging above the valve. The third issue is air valve vents. Again, if you have not been trained in how it is designed to work, the vent can and will plug—and if the vent plugs, the same issues seen with clearance issues will result. The fourth and final issue with air valves is the packing, again a misunderstood item. Like it or not, your air valve packing will leak, or should leak, a small amount of material (less than a pound a day). The most common problem occurs when someone over-tightens the packing; this will result in abrasive erosion of the valve shaft—or worse if tightened when the valve is not running: motor overload or drive chain breakage. Wear of the drive shaft again results in air and product leaks, affecting the efficiency of the conveyance system.

    Good maintenance begins with education. I strongly recommend that if you have a pneumatic conveyance system and rotary air valves, contact your air valve vendor and have them come in and provide training on the proper installation and maintenance of these components. As I stated above, there is only ONE correct way to install a rotary air valve. Here are the three things to look for:

    - Is the valve feed-side up? In many cases this is difficult to determine. If your air valve is vented, the vent connection should be facing up, not down. If the conveyor vent is not facing in the correct direction, the vent will plug and air will discharge to the feed side of the valve.

    - Is the valve turning in the correct direction? Check the endplate on the valve, and you should see an arrow. That arrow should point in the direction of air/product flow.

- Are the valve vanes oriented correctly? The vane blade should be parallel to the conveyor piping, so when the product dumps into the pipe, the airflow cleans the entire cavity out.

Perform daily rounds to inspect air valve packing glands for leaks greater than a pound a day. (Show your inspector what a pound of product looks like.) Develop a good job plan for packing maintenance that includes the correct type, how to correctly replace and stagger packing, and how to tighten the packing gland. Regarding the air valve vent, the easiest way to ensure the vent is working properly is with a pressure gauge. There should be no pressure on the vent; if pressure is noted, the vent is plugged. Beyond these tasks it is a good idea to have an annual inspection of the drive chain for stretching and of the sprockets for wear. Measure stretch, and use a sprocket gauge to determine wear. Replace each based on set standards.

Two rotary air valves, or rotary air locks, feeding a conveyor belt. Have you trained your maintenance technicians to properly install these assets to improve the efficiency of your system?

6. **Cyclone Separators:** Generally the last place I look when a pneumatic conveyance system is suffering from performance or efficiency issues, the cyclone separator is a static piece of equipment that should be very reliable. There are, however, two issues I have seen that can result in system problems. The first is erosion where the product enters the cyclone and spins rapidly before dropping out of the air stream. Over

time this will lead to thinning of the separator walls and eventually result in air and dust leaks. The second is caking of wet product or dust to the cyclone walls. This will result in reduced ability to quickly drop product and dust from the air stream and carry over to the dust collector. This typically becomes evident through filter bag plugging and high differential pressure across the dust collector tube sheet. Your maintenance strategy here should be quite simple. Perform uniform thickness testing of the dust collector walls to determine the rate of erosion, and perform visual internal inspection of the cyclone walls if you have experienced frequent plugging of dust collector bags.

7. **Dust Collectors:** While the concept, design, and operation of a dust collector is relatively simple, dust collectors are typically the assets within the pneumatic conveyance system that require the most maintenance. I will also point out, however, that in most cases we create our own maintenance issues by allowing the system efficiency to drop and by damaging the dust collector components during maintenance. The key issues with dust collectors are the filter bags, filter cages, nozzle (if your cages are bottom loaded), tube sheet, blow downs, and door seals. A properly designed and maintained dust collector should operate without issues for at least six months at a time. If you are opening the system to clean bags more often than this, chances are your system efficiency is no longer in balance. Looking at each of the items I listed above, I will now describe the most common problems for each:

Dust collector bags: It is highly important that the bags you are using in your dust collector were designed to filter the material you are running in your system. All dust collector bags are not created equal; using the wrong bag can lead to bag plugging or dust leakage. The most common issue with the filter bags is torn or damaged bags resulting from personnel knocking down the bags. This, of course, leads to dust leaking through the clean side of the filter and out to the atmosphere, or dust coming back to the fan in closed-loop systems. The last common issue is improper installation of the bags, and this again leads to dust leakage.

Filter Cages: If your system is operating properly, the filter cages should rarely be an issue. On a system I worked with that was suffering from performance and efficiency issues at Eastman Kodak, the bags and filters were being knocked down and cleaned weekly. As a result, this added to the problem and affected the reliability of the entire system. Once we identified the specific issues that caused the plugging and corrected these issues, the filter bags lasted five years and the cages never had to be replaced. Knocking down bags results in damage to the filter cages, and damaged cages always end up with a torn bag or the entire cage falling off.

Filter Cage Nozzles: Again, these should never be an issue, but if your system is out of control and you are knocking down your filter bags in attempt to clean them, plan on damaging the cage nozzle.

Dust Collector Tube Sheet: Depending on your dust collector design, I have seen only two issues here. The first is if the tube sheet is bolted to a support ring, it is possible for the seal/gasket to leak. The second is for welded tube sheets (not a huge fan). More often than not, the welds will crack and leak as a result of thermal expansion and the flexing of the tube sheet that occurs in normal operation of the system. Both items lead to dust leaking through to the clean side and out to the atmosphere—which, by the way, creates an explosion hazard at your site.

Blow Downs: The blow downs in a dust collector are installed to create a quick burst of high-velocity air that is intended to clean dust off the bag on the dirty, or high-pressure side, of the tube sheet. The two big issues with blow downs result from improper installation and solenoid valve failure. Improper installation of the blow downs results in the inability to clean dust from the filter bags. Plugged bags, in turn, will lead to reduced airflow and loss of system performance and efficiency. Failure of the blow down solenoids results in the loss of your blow down air supply, and again your bags will plug.

Door Seals/Gaskets: If you open and close your dust collector over and over again, plan on the door seal leaking. At this point your ability to filter the dust will be affected, and dust will leak from the high-pressure side of the unit to the atmosphere.

Dust Collector Maintenance: This starts with understanding how the dust collector works with your conveyance system. Continuously monitor the differential pressure across your tube sheet. If your system is working properly, the differential pressure should remain consistent for weeks and months at a time. For this reason I often recommend that we provide a signal to the PLC where we can trend and alarm differential pressure. The second thing that we need the PLC to monitor is the function of the blow down solenoid valves. It is highly important to know that each valve opens and closes at the set interval as one valve can control the air to several bags. If the solenoid fails to actuate, maintenance will need to know and take action as soon as possible

Filter Bag, Cage, and Nozzle Maintenance: DON'T hit the bags and cages to knock dust off! This only creates more issues. Determine why the bags have plugged and resolve that issue. Make sure the bags in your dust collector were designed to filter the media being conveyed in your system. Have your bag supplier verify that you have the correct bags and provide training on how to properly install the bags and cages.

Dust Collector Tube Sheet Maintenance: Maintenance is quite simple in this case. Visually inspect the clean side of your dust collector for evidence of dust at bag changes. While there will often be a small amount of dust (or a large amount if the bags are torn), look at the tube sheet gaskets and welds for evidence of blow through. On very clean systems I have used a strobe light to view dust leaking by gaskets and at cracked welds.

Door Gasket Maintenance: Keep the door closed unless you plan to replace the filter bags. When you do open and close the door, inspect the gasket for evidence of cracking or embrittlement and replace the gasket if noted.

A large pneumatic conveyance system dust collector. Most problems with pneumatic conveyance systems stem from improper training, neglect, and abuse of the dust collector. Operating your system at its best efficiency point can be achieved only by understanding how this system was designed to operate, learning how to diagnose or identify when the system is operating out of control, and developing sound operating and maintenance procedures to ensure reliability and efficiency.

Closing out this chapter, I would like to state that having worked with dozens of pneumatic conveyance systems of various designs and sizes that conveyed several different types of materials, I am continually amazed by one thing: how these systems continue to run as they are operated well outside of the designed best efficiency point. In most cases, by the time I have been contacted to perform an RCM analysis of a conveyor system, it has suffered multiple failures and efficiency is the least of the company's concerns. In reality, pneumatic conveyance systems are very reliable and will operate with very few noticeable issues with a loss of efficiency as high as 30%. But such a loss in efficiency is costing your company a lot of money in wasted energy and product losses. In other words, if it should take you one hour to convey a bin of product from point A to point B, it will now take you nearly one hour and 20 minutes. Time is money. It's lost production and wasted energy. If you maintain this system and keep it reliable, the payback is a triple play: You won't have down time, you won't be spending money on failed components, and you won't have the additional energy costs that come with running an inefficient system.

The last recommendation is one I will make for a second time: Go to the International Powder and Bulk Solids Conference!

Reference Notes:

1. Kenneth Hellevang, "Pneumatic Grain Conveyors," http://www.ag.ndsu.nodak.edu/abeng/pdffiles/ae850.pdf.

2. Department of Energy, "Improving Fan System Performance: A Sourcebook for Industry," http://www1.eere.energy.gov/industry/ bestpractices/pdfs/fan_sourcebook.pdf.

3. International Powder and Bulk Solids Conference, http://www.thomex.com/trade-events/powder-and-bulk- solids-2010-2130.html.

Chapter 6

Compressed Air Systems

When it comes to wasting energy in manufacturing, compressed air may be king. I would offer a guess that I have performed no less than 10 RCM Blitz™ analyses on compressed air systems, and those that were implemented were successful. While compressed air systems on their own typically don't yield what I would call a multimillion-dollar RCM home run—improved reliability, increased throughput, and lower maintenance costs—a finely tuned and reliable compressed air system will result in significant energy savings that will improve your company's bottom line.

There is one huge problem with the reliability of compressed air systems, and that problem is people.

What we typically see with compressed air systems is a design and installation that when new delivered dry compressed air at a desired volume and pressure in a reliable fashion for a number of years. With this new system your company was handed an OEM (Original Equipment Manufacturer) manual, and from this guide you may or may not have set up some basic preventive maintenance tasks to help keep this critical asset in like-new condition. The nice part about compressed air systems is that most manufacturing companies use compressed air, so over the years the companies that manufacture these systems know what it takes to properly design, size, and install a system that should offer a high level of reliability. The key word here is should! Having analyzed the failure modes for several compressed air systems over the past 15 years, I can safely say that there is one huge problem with the reliability of compressed air systems, and that problem is people.

A compressed air system like the one pictured above is a critical asset when it comes to the reliability of your plant. If taken for granted and under-maintained, it will in no time begin operating out of control, costing your company tens of thousands of dollars in energy losses and hundreds of thousands of dollars in lost production and additional maintenance costs!

It would seem that from the day we install our plant's compressed air system, we then begin working as a team to ignore, neglect, abuse, and destroy this once-reliable asset until it can no longer deliver its intended function.

Compressed air systems are quite simple in design and purpose—so much so that one would wonder just how we end up with something that is so unreliable and inefficient. The cycle of abuse typically starts with air leaks. I have yet to work on a compressed air system that did not have significant air loss due to leakage. Lost air is wasted energy; it takes a significant amount of electricity to produce compressed air, so any air that leaks from the system without first being used to perform a specific function is wasted money. While this seems to come with a simple solution, I have visited more than 1,000 plants in my travels, and I can count on one hand the number of plants that have PdM tasks in place to detect and repair compressed air leaks.

Looking simply at air leaks alone, UE Systems reports that companies that do not have a maintenance program in place to detect compressed air leaks will lose a minimum of 20% of the compressed air they generate. Using basic logic, if we were to identify and repair compressed air leaks, we could reduce energy usage on this system by 20%. For a general idea of how much compressed air leaks cost, review the following tables.

Discharge of Air Through an Orifice
In cubic feet of free air per minute, at standard atmospheric pressure of 14.7 psi absolute and 70°F.

Gauge Pressure Before Orifice in PSI	1/64"	1/32"	1/16"	1/8"	1/4"	3/8"	1/2"	5/8"	3/4"	7/8"	1"
1	0.028	0.112	0.45	1.80	7.18	16.20	28.70	45.00	64.70	88.10	115.00
2	0.040	0.158	0.63	2.53	10.10	22.80	40.50	63.30	91.20	124.00	162.00
3	0.048	0.194	0.78	3.10	12.40	27.80	49.50	77.50	111.00	152.00	198.00
4	0.056	0.223	0.89	3.56	14.30	32.10	57.00	89.20	128.00	175.00	228.00
5	0.062	0.248	0.99	3.97	15.90	35.70	63.50	99.30	143.00	195.00	254.00
6	0.068	0.272	1.09	4.34	17.40	39.10	69.50	109.00	156.00	213.00	278.00
7	0.073	0.293	1.17	4.68	18.70	42.20	75.00	117.00	168.00	230.00	300.00
9	0.083	0.331	1.32	5.30	21.20	47.70	84.70	132.00	191.00	260.00	339.00
12	0.095	0.379	1.52	6.07	24.30	54.60	97.00	152.00	218.00	297.00	388.00
15	0.105	0.420	1.68	6.72	26.90	60.50	108.00	168.00	242.00	329.00	430.00
20	0.123	0.491	1.96	7.86	31.40	70.70	126.00	196.00	283.00	385.00	503.00
25	0.140	0.562	2.25	8.98	35.90	80.90	144.00	225.00	323.00	440.00	575.00
30	0.158	0.633	2.53	10.10	40.50	91.10	162.00	253.00	365.00	496.00	648.00
35	0.176	0.703	2.81	11.30	45.00	101.00	180.00	281.00	405.00	551.00	720.00
40	0.194	0.774	3.10	12.40	49.60	112.00	198.00	310.00	446.00	607.00	793.00
45	0.211	0.845	3.38	13.50	54.10	122.00	216.00	338.00	487.00	662.00	865.00
50	0.229	0.916	3.66	14.70	58.60	132.00	235.00	366.00	528.00	718.00	938.00
60	0.264	1.060	4.23	16.90	67.60	152.00	271.00	423.00	609.00	828.00	1082.00
70	0.300	1.200	4.79	19.20	76.70	173.00	307.00	479.00	690.00	939.00	1371.00
80	0.335	1.340	5.36	21.40	85.70	193.00	343.00	536.00	771.00	1050.00	2023.00
90	0.370	1.480	5.92	23.70	94.80	213.00	379.00	592.00	853.00	1161.00	1516.00
100	0.406	1.620	6.49	26.00	104.00	234.00	415.00	649.00	934.00	1272.00	1661.00
110	0.441	1.760	7.05	28.20	113.00	254.00	452.00	705.00	1016.00	1383.00	1806.00
120	0.476	1.910	7.62	30.50	122.00	274.00	488.00	762.00	1097.00	1494.00	1951.00
125	0.494	1.980	7.90	31.60	126.00	284.00	506.00	790.00	1138.00	1549.00	2023.00
150	0.582	2.370	9.45	37.50	150.00	338.00	600.00	910.00	1315.00	1789.00	2338.00
200	0.761	3.100	12.35	49.00	196.00	441.00	784.00	1225.00	1764.00	2401.00	3136.00
250	0.935	3.800	15.18	60.30	241.00	542.00	964.00	1508.00	2169.00	2952.00	3856.00
300	0.995	4.880	18.08	71.80	278.00	646.00	1148.00	1795.00	2583.00	3515.00	4592.00
400	1.220	5.980	23.81	94.50	378.00	851.00	1512.00	2360.00	3402.00	4630.00	6048.00
500	1.519	7.410	29.55	117.30	469.00	1055.00	1876.00	2930.00	4221.00	5745.00	7504.00
750	2.240	10.980	43.85	174.00	696.00	1566.00	2784.00	4350.00	6264.00	8525.00	11136.00
1000	2.985	14.600	58.21	231.00	924.00	2079.00	3696.00	5790.00	8316.00	11318.00	14784.00

The above table is based on 100% coefficient of flow. For well-rounded entrance, multiply values by .97. For sharp-edged orifices, a multiplier of 0.61 may be used for approximate results. Values for pressures from 1 to 15 lbs. gauge calculated by standard adiabatic formula. Values for pressures above 15 lbs. gauge calculated by approximate formula proposed by S.A. Moss. Table provided by UE Systems Inc.

Air Leak Cost					
Diameter of Leak	Cubic Feet/ Min	Cubic Feet/Day	Loss/Day Dollars	Loss/Month Dollars	Loss/Year Dollars
1/64"	.45	576	$0.13	$4.00	$48.00
1/32"	1.60	2,304	$0.51	$15.50	$186.00
3/64"	3.66	5,270	$1.16	$35.30	$424.00
1/16"	6.45	9,288	$2.04	$62.00	$744.00
3/32"	14.50	20,880	$4.59	$139.50	$1,674.00
1/8"	25.80	37,152	$8.17	$248.40	$2,981.00
3/16"	58.30	83,952	$18.47	$561.50	$6,738.00
1/4"	103.00	148,320	$32.63	$992.00	$11,904.00
5/16"	162.00	233,280	$51.32	$1,560.00	$18,721.00
3/8"	234.00	336,960	$74.13	$2,253.60	$27,036.00

Based on 100 psig; $0.22/MCF; 8,760 hours/year • Cost table provided by UE Systems Inc.

How to Calculate Your CFM Loss as Dollar Loss Per Year
Provided by UE Systems Inc.

The basic calculation of a leak's costs in terms of CFM can be determined by using the following formula:

$$\frac{(CFM \times 60)\ (8760) \times MCF}{1000} = \text{Leak Cost Per Year}$$

1. Convert your CFM into cubic feet/hour
   CFM x 60
   Example: 3.6 CFM x 60 = 216 cubic feet per hour

2. Calculate cubic feet per year. Multiply the number of hours the system is in use by the hourly figure.
   Example: 216 x 8760 (hours per year) = 1,892,160 cubic feet per year

3. To determine the cost per year, determine the cost of compressed air. This is usually represented by MCF (Thousand Cubic Feet). First, divide the hourly figure by 1,000, and then multiply by the MCF cost figure.
   Example: MCF cost is $0.22
   1,892,160 / 1000 = 1,892.16
   1,892.16 x $0.22 = $416.28 cost per year

The above photo shows an airborne ultrasound technician locating compressed air leaks. Identifying, tagging, repairing, and calculating the savings from repairing air leaks will save your company money and ensure the reliability of your compressed air system.

Now that we have addressed the cost of compressed air leaks and the energy efficiency gains we could expect from having a leak-tight system, let's look at the reliability issues that result from ignoring this system.

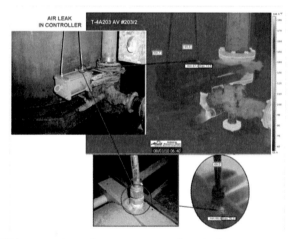

The infrared (IR) image above shows a compressed air leak at a compression fitting on this pneumatic cylinder. While IR is not the preferred PdM method for locating air leaks, one of our PdM techs was kind enough to send me this photo illustrating what a significant air leak looks like. As he was walking through this area, he could hear a large air leak and was able to locate it with his camera.

As compressed air is wasted through leaks, we should be able to see the first signs of overtaxing the design by simply looking at the volume of compressed air being produced if we were trending this in our PLC or DCS. A steady increase in volume produced by the system might be the first indication that the system is leaking. (I would add that using airborne ultrasonic leak detection would detect leakage long before it would show on a volume or flow trend.) Overtaxing this system results in some severe long-term effects, and many of these of these will go undetected until the system is out of control and operational losses are eminent. It should be noted that this slippery slope is often compounded as our business grows and we add additional assets that consume compressed air. As we add new manufacturing equipment, we rarely consider additional maintenance resources. As a result, we lose focus on the importance of our building air system and become lax in completing important PM and PdM tasks on this system. At some point in time the volume of air being generated will exceed the designed capacity of the air dryer system. Once this occurs, the air dryer unit will no longer be able to fully regenerate; it will cycle back and forth between the two dryer towers. If you have properly programmed your compressed air system, your operators should be alarmed when the operating dew point can no longer be maintained. It should also be noted that every time the dryer towers cycle, we use a significant amount of energy to regenerate each dryer tower. At this point we have a critical decision to make:

1. You can ignore the alarm and keep production running.

2. You can reset the alarm and very quickly begin a plan to bring this system back into control.

If you don't select Option 2, be prepared to see the impact that wet and compressed air has on the reliability of every component that operates with compressed air. Solenoid valves will begin to stick; air filters will plug; air-operated control valves will drift, react slowly, and cycle; and if your equipment is in an environment where air temperatures fall below freezing, be prepared for hundreds of hours of thawing out frozen air lines!

*Identifying, tagging, and repairing compressed air leaks will keep
your air clean, your air dryers (pictured above) operating in control,
and save your company a significant amount of money.*

As I began working on this chapter, I could not help remembering one particular RCM analysis we performed for a customer. After listing the main and support functions for the system and components, the team decided to take a quick tour of the compressor room to make sure we hadn't missed any components. As we prepared to enter the compressor room, I noticed the first sign of neglect: Both compressors were running, and parts of the intake filters were hanging down and flapping away in the intake piping. It became very clear that we were about to perform an RCM analysis for a critical asset that was on its deathbed! The compressor room was loud, dirty, and hot. Oil and water were leaking from the compressor oil coolers, and the water trap solenoid was stuck open on one of the air dryers, releasing a 1/2" stream of 100 psig air straight down toward the floor. It had been leaking long enough that the concrete below had eroded a hole large enough to consume a golf ball. We looked around the room for nearly 10 minutes, pointing at visible problems but unable to converse over the noise. Upon exiting I asked our host, "So, what made you pick the compressed air system as your first RCM analysis?" With a straight face he replied, "Well, we have been having some problems with the system. It can't keep up, and as a result we have had two major losses in our manufacturing equipment in the last month. Last week we seized one of the compressors and installed our spare. The rebuild of the old compressor won't be done for six weeks, so we ordered a portable unit and installed that around the corner. We now have three compressors running and we are still having problems. We are really hoping that this RCM will help us get back in control."

Nothing like big expectations!

The RCM analysis took a week to complete. We addressed 165 failure modes, which resulted in more than 230 tasks. Implementation of the tasks was a challenge. It turns out that their system had been out of control for several years, and the main air headers and branches had severely eroded from wet, dirty air and needed to be replaced. The screens in both air dryers had collapsed, and the desiccant had turned to hardened powder. Over the next six months they spent hundreds of man-hours and tens of thousands of dollars to bring the system back in control. In the end, with the leaks repaired and major components back to new condition, they once again were able to run the entire plant on a single compressor. I am happy to report that seven years later they are still running on a single compressor and complete over 95% of their air system PM and PdM tasks each year.

Think back and imagine the money and energy wasted as a result of ignoring this critical system!

A quick list of suggestions for existing energy-efficient compressed air systems:

1. If you are considering adding new manufacturing equipment to your plant, make sure you run the calculations for the amount of air you are presently using and the requirements of your new equipment. Ensure that your existing system can handle the new load.

2. Every company that has a compressed air system should be using an airborne ultrasonic instrument to detect leaks and work on a regular basis to keep air leaks to a minimum. Check all leak points on a quarterly basis, and when leaks are detected make sure they get repaired.

3. Make sure the compressors and motors are precision aligned each time they are uncoupled and re-coupled for maintenance.

4. Set a standard for equipment vibration and make sure the compressor and motor operate within that standard.

5. Educate the people who work in your plant on the costs of compressed air and the impact that compressed air has on the reliability of your production assets.

6. Closely monitor compressed air usage, dew point, and differential pressure across the intake filters. Install the instruments and program alarm points.

Suggestions for designing a reliable compressed air system:

1. Be sure to design your new system with plant growth in mind.

2. Most new compressed air systems are skid mount units; should this be the case for your new design, make sure to create requirement documents for both alignment and vibration, and make the vendor guarantee that the new equipment will meet or exceed these standards.

3. Keep the number of leak points to a minimum in your design. Create a requirements document for the company installing your system that guarantees a leak-free system at start-up.

4. Make sure your new system has the instruments necessary to monitor the health of your compressed air system and that the system can be controlled, or at a minimum install alarms in your operations control room. Items I would like to continuously monitor and alarm:

   • Air pressure
   • Airflow
   • Air usage
   • Dew point
   • Compressor vibration
   • Regeneration cycle

5. Ensure all compressed air system alarms provide a clear indication of the problem. (No general alarms!)

6. As a general rule, it's a good idea to disconnect tool air hoses that are not in use. Quick connects of all types have a tendency to leak, so when they are not in use, valve the air to the hose station off or disconnect the hose.

7. Eliminate all inappropriate uses of compressed air. We often see compressed air being used to blow off dirt or dust from photo eyes or as a means to dry product. In most cases there are more efficient ways to accomplish this without taxing the compressed air system.

Chapter 7

Refrigeration Systems

Refrigeration systems are very similar to HVAC systems in that most are suitable for changes in design and maintenance practices that will have a direct impact on the reliability and energy efficiency of the asset. Probably because refrigeration systems are a key element in most HVAC systems, they are seen as a utility, and people as a rule want comfort and functionality over efficiency. We simply want utilities to work, and when they do we forget about them. Refrigeration systems are composed of some combination of condensers, compressors, evaporators, valves, absorbers, pumps, and chillers. As we will discuss, many opportunities exist to optimize the efficiency of these varied components.

Probably because refrigeration systems are a key element in most HVAC systems, they are seen as a utility, and people as a rule want comfort and functionality over efficiency.

When I began researching energy-efficiency improvements for refrigeration systems, I began with the American Society of Heating, Refrigeration and Air-Conditioning Engineers (ASHRAE). They have a lot of information available on their website focusing on technology to serve humanity and promote a sustainable world. Not only will you find articles, case studies, and examples of technological advances improving the efficiency of refrigeration systems, but also you will also be able to obtain copies of the latest ASHRAE Standards and Guidelines. ASHRAE writes standards for the purpose of establishing a consensus for: 1) methods of test for use in commerce and 2) performance criteria for use as facilitators with which to guide the industry. ASHRAE publishes the following three types of voluntary consensus standards: Method of Measurement or Test, Standard Design, and Standard Practice. *The ASHRAE Handbook*, a series of four volumes, is a great resource when dealing with HVAC and refrigeration systems. The four volumes are: *2007 ASHRAE Handbook – HVAC Applications*, *2008 ASHRAE Handbook – HVAC Systems and Equipment*, *2009 ASHRAE Handbook – Fundamentals*, and *2010 ASHRAE Handbook – Refrigeration*.

Air conditioning is typically used to remove heat from an occupied space and maintain the space at a temperature lower than the outdoor or surrounding temperature. This process requires the use of a refrigeration system. In simple terms, a refrigeration machine absorbs heat from the cold body at temperature T1 and releases the heat H1 into the surroundings at temperature T2. This process requires work to be done on the system. The heat released into the surroundings equals the heat absorbed from the cold body plus the work done or mechanical energy consumed. To accomplish this function, refrigerants are used in the refrigeration machines. Refrigerants evaporate at low temperatures and condense at higher temperatures, which allows them to be used to absorb the heat during the evaporation and then release it into the atmosphere when condensed.

Let's start by explaining the two most common refrigeration cycles used: vapor compression and absorption. Basic configurations of these cycles are shown below:

Typical Vapor-Compression Cycle

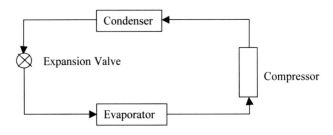

Typical Absorption Cycle

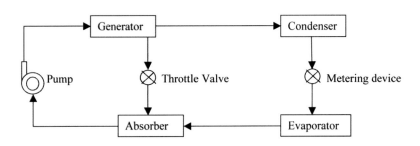

By far, the most common process for producing cooling for buildings is the vapor-compression refrigeration cycle. It has four main mechanical components through which the refrigerant is circulated in a closed loop as shown in the diagram above. Essentially the design is to move heat from a controlled environment to a warmer, uncontrolled environment through the evaporation of a refrigerant driven through the refrigeration cycle by a compressor.

Another refrigeration cycle is the absorption cycle. This cycle is heat-driven, unlike the vapor compression cycle, which is work-driven. The absorption cycle uses heat energy to drive the refrigerant cycle, extracting heat from a controlled environment and ejecting it into the environment. This cycle typically involves a mixture of two substances, such as ammonia and water or lithium bromide and water, that attract each other. Absorption chillers are seldom used anymore because of their poor coefficient of performance (COP) and significant use of water for cooling tower evaporation. Absorption chillers are effectively used only when there is a waste heat stream from some other process, which would normally be rejected but can be used to power the absorption chiller. It is almost always an attractive energy conservation opportunity to replace the absorber with a highly efficient electrical centrifugal machine, unless it is utilizing wasted heat or a cheap source of heat.

Chillers are the biggest energy consumers in central air-conditioning systems. Chillers normally work on the vapor compression cycle or the absorption cycle. Since electric chillers working on the vapor compression cycle are the most common, and significant energy savings can be achieved from these machines through various energy management strategies, the remaining portion of this chapter will be devoted to chillers and their operation.

Let's first assume we have the opportunity to design, build, and install the perfect, most efficient cooling system. While many of us may not have the opportunity to be involved at this stage, it is at this stage that many opportunities exist to build the foundation for sustainability. In the design and implementation phase, there are nine foundational elements to consider. These elements are divided into two sections as shown on the next page:

Reduce Cooling Demand

- Eliminate requirement to cool entire space equally
- Expand the comfort envelope
- Minimize sources of heat and humidity gains
- Optimize balance-of-plant (pumps, piping loops, etc.)

Select Cooling Approach

- Apply passive cooling techniques
- Consider active non-refrigerative cooling techniques
- Use super-efficient refrigerative technology (COP > 5.8)
- Optimize automation controls and operation
- Capture beneficial by-products

OK, to stay on topic, let's assume we are using some type of chiller(s) for our refrigeration system. There are basically two types—air cooled and water cooled—which typically are classified according to the type of compressor used for the refrigerant. There are four main types of compressors used: reciprocating, scroll, screw, and centrifugal. The compressor type that is chosen will depend on the application and desired performance of the refrigeration system. Reciprocating and centrifugal compressors are generally good for high-capacity applications, while scroll and screw compressors are generally better designed for lower-capacity applications.

As with most equipment, there are important specifications to consider when choosing industrial chillers. Such specifications include total life cycle cost, power source, cooling capacity, evaporator capacity, condenser capacity, fluid discharge temperature, process flow, process pressure, reservoir capacity, coolant requirements, and efficiency or COP.

Chiller efficiency is measured in terms of how many units of power are used to produce one unit of cooling.

$$Chiller\ Efficiency = Power\ input \div Cooling\ produced$$

In the English IP system, chiller efficiency is measured in kW/RT.

$$where\ kW/RT = \frac{kW\ input}{Tons\ of\ refrigeration}$$

In the SI metric system, chiller efficiency is measured in coefficient of performance (COP).

$$where\ COP = \frac{kW\ refrigeration\ effect}{kW\ input}$$

$$kW\ refrigeration\ effect = RT * 3.517$$

The energy efficiency ratio (EER), which is the ratio of the cooling capacity (Btu/h) to the electric power input (W), is often used to rate reciprocating and scroll compressors in air-cooled chillers and direct-expansion refrigeration units.

Since chiller efficiency varies with loading, it is usually rated at full-load (100% of rated capacity) and part-load conditions (90%, 80%, 70%, and so on). This information, normally provided by the manufacturer, is useful in selecting chillers to maximize efficiency based on application.

In fact, there are two things that have a great impact on the energy efficiency of a refrigeration system. One is the type of refrigerant that is used. For example, ammonia is a very light refrigerant with a high energy content, which makes it very efficient. The other item that has a great impact on the energy efficiency of the refrigeration system is the use of a reciprocating compressor in combination with a flooded system. Although reciprocating compressors are often considered old-fashioned, they offer much better efficiencies than compact screws. At part load, the reciprocating compressor will keep the efficiency, whereas the screw becomes less efficient.

As mentioned previously, chillers seldom operate at full load. The part-load performance has an enormous effect on the total average power consumption. For American climatic conditions we utilize a standard called "ARI standard 550/590 IPLV." This standard specifies an average COP for one year and makes it easy to compare the power consumption of different chillers and the application they may be used for. The table on the next page shows the typical efficiencies for both water-cooled and air-cooled chillers:

Chiller Efficiencies			
Air-cooled (including condenser power >150 tons)	EER	COP	kW/ton
ASHRAE Standard 90.1 1999	9.6	2.8	1.26
Good	9.9	2.9	1.21
Best	10.6	3.1	1.13
Water-cooled (>300 ton centrifugal compressor)	EER	COP	KW/ton
ASHRAE Code 90.1 1999	16.7	4.9	0.72
Good	18.5	5.4	0.65
Best	26.7	7.8	0.45

In the foundational elements listed previously in the "Select Cooling Approach" section, we have listed "Optimize automation controls and operation." This is a major item for consideration, as discussed in a recent paper presented at the 2010 Industrial Refrigeration Conference & Exhibition. *(Ref. 1)* In Sergei Khoudiachov's abstract, he states, "For years, many professional engineers focused on the design of energy efficient refrigeration plants. Although a well-designed refrigeration plant is the foundation of energy savings, the efficient operation of a refrigeration plant is the ultimate goal of the energy saving process in industrial refrigeration. Through efficient operation, up to 70–80% of total energy savings can be achieved." How we operate our refrigeration systems greatly impacts the efficiencies we are able to obtain. Khoudiachov discusses this topic in great detail and categorizes "Key Energy Saving Measures" to address this issue. Following you will find a summary of these measures:

Optimum Condensing Pressure	•"Float" condensing pressure at optimum level to minimize energy based on operating environment (seasonal changes, etc.). •Barriers to operating at low condensing pressures: hot gas defrosting, liquid supply, oil carryover.
Optimum Suction Pressure	•Raising suction pressure improves compressor efficiency (1–2% per 1°F increase in suction temperature). •Keep in mind, to determine a system's optimum suction pressure, the efficiency of the whole refrigeration plant should be evaluated.
Optimized Hot Gas Defrosting	•Significant energy losses can be contributed to the wrong frequency of hot gas defrosting. •Criteria of optimization must be chosen.
Optimized Compressor Sequence	•Determine reasons for load fluctuation before adjusting compressor sequencing.
Use of VFDs	•If a plant is poorly designed and/or poorly operated, energy losses will likely be great and can be recovered through the use of VFDs.
Remote Tuning Up	•Tune to optimize operation. •Critical to determine optimum set points and optimum operating strategies.

Useful Refrigeration System Maintenance

1. Perform an annual PM inspection of the compressor to ensure proper operation. (The specifics of PM will vary depending on the type of compressor and system configuration.) Items may include:

   a. Air temperature (e.g., high air temperature could be caused by inadequate cooling of the air, which will overheat the compressor).

   b. Check for proper oil level and temperature to verify operation of oil pump, filter, and screen.

   c. Air pressure control verification. This check will verify whether the compressor is unloading and loading when in continuous operation. Poor output pressure could indicate valve problems or control valve malfunction.

   d. Safety valve check. Verify that the safety valve is not leaking because of over-pressure or failure of device.

e. Filter cleanliness check. This check should be done to avoid having dirt enter the system and decreased efficiency due to high pressure drop over the air filter. Filters should be clean and free of debris. When pressure drop across the filter is significantly different than initial values, filters should be replaced. Generally, pressure drop across filters should be no more than 5 psi (34 kPa).

f. Automatic moisture trap verification. When air cools in the system, water tends to precipitate and if not removed will contaminate the entire system. The automatic drain traps should be functioning properly to prevent this defect. The bypass valve should be manually opened to verify that water runs out.

g. Check the entire compressor area for leaks, including hoses, fittings, foundation, filters, etc. No signs of air, water, oil, or refrigerant leakage should be present. If leaks are present, locate and report the source of the leak.

2. Routine PdM or CBM routes should be in place to detect many of the above defects.

a. IR thermography should be utilized on a quarterly basis to determine any temperature anomalies, insulation issues, piping or process conditions, and leakage.

b. Motor Circuit Analysis should be utilized on a biannual basis to evaluate the six fault zones for all motors installed in the system.

c. Vibration analysis should be utilized on a monthly basis to determine structural, mechanical, and electrical faults of the rotating components.

d. Oil analysis should be utilized on a quarterly basis to ensure that contamination does not occur.

e. Airborne ultrasound should be utilized on a quarterly basis to check for leaks and other mechanical rotating defects.

In closing, it should be mentioned that contamination is one of the major defects of refrigeration systems. When a chiller operates with contaminated refrigerant, performance will decline, power use increases, and operating costs have the potential to increase exponentially. Contamination can be air, oil, moisture, dirt, or acid. If not detected and addressed, it can cause catastrophic damage.

The most common contaminant in refrigerants is oil. A recent ASHRAE research project (601-TRP) sampled refrigerant from ten randomly selected chillers and concluded that all contained excess oil even though three of them had recently had their refrigerant recycled. Of the ones that were recycled, the study showed oil content of 3–7% in the refrigerant. The other seven samples showed contamination levels ranging from 9% to more than 20%. The table below shows approximately how energy efficiency declines as excess oil builds.

How Energy Efficiency Declines As Excess Oil Builds	
Percent Oil in Evaporator	**Energy Efficiency Loss**
• 1 Percent to 2 Percent	• 2 Percent to 4 Percent
• 3 Percent to 4 Percent	• 5.5 Percent to 8 Percent
• 5 Percent to 6 Percent	• 9.5 Percent to 11 Percent
• 7 Percent to 8 Percent	• 13.5 Percent to 15 Percent
Because oil usually accumulates gradually in refrigerant through migraton, the attendant loss in efficiency usually is diagnosed to be some other cause. It isn't until performance has significantly degraded that oil is suspected.	

Now, typically little is done to identify and remove excess oil from chillers until it becomes a major problem. Why is this? Well, because oil on the refrigerant side typically does no damage to the system, gives little indication of its presence, and generally has significant costs associated with detection. It typically isn't until performance has significantly degraded that oil is suspected.

Water and acid contamination is the most dangerous refrigerant contamination. Moisture in the refrigerant side presents one of the most common and costly problems to a chiller. Not only will such contamination reduce chiller efficiency, but it also creates serious damage in several components. Undetected, moisture can lead to significant downtime and repair expense. Moisture can:

- Form as ice in expansion valves, capillary tubes, and evaporators.

- Combine with lubricating oil in the compressor to form acids that attack the motor windings, leading to burnout.

- Remove copper ions from tubing and deposit them on hot surfaces, causing bearings to seize.

- Join with oil to form a sludge that blocks oil flow passages, pits polished surfaces, and restricts metering devices.

- Significantly reduce chiller efficiency.

Air is one of the most difficult contaminants to remove from a chiller or refrigeration system. If left in the refrigerant side, this non-condensable can cause excessive head pressure and higher operating temperatures and result in higher utility costs, degradation of lubricant effectiveness, and premature compressor problems.

Fortunately, there are many solutions to combat these kinds of contaminants, such as purge units that are retrofitted to the chillers. Such purge units are specific for the removal of all contaminants. In process heating applications where cooling is required and where lost production can cost a fortune, these purge units make solid sense. *(Ref. 2)*

Reference Notes:

1. Sergei Khoudiachov, S K Energy Consulting Ltd., "Optimization of Refrigeration Plant Operation Engineering Approach," technical papers for International Institute of Ammonia Refrigeration, 32nd Annual Meeting, March 14–17, 2010.

2. Mark Key, Redi Controls Inc., "Maintain Chiller Capacity and Efficiency," article for *Process Heating for Manufacturing Engineers*, August 1, 2007.

Other Sources:

Lal Jayamaha, *Energy-Efficient Building Systems: Green Strategies for Operations and Maintenance*, McGraw-Hill, 2007.

Allied Reliability Inc., *PM/PdM Electrical, Mechanical, and Stationary Best Practices*.

Department of Energy, Building Technologies Program, http://www1.eere.energy.gov/buildings/.

Steve Doty and Wayne C. Turner, *Energy Management Handbook*, Fairmont Press, 2009, 7th ed.

American Society of Heating, Refrigerating and Air-Conditioning Engineers http://www.ashrae.org/.

Chapter 8

Hydraulic Systems

As a mechanic, I never liked working on hydraulic systems. They were dirty, oily, smelly, and slippery. If you were working on a hydraulic system, everyone in the break room knew it the minute you walked through the door. If it wasn't the stink, it was the attitude.

When I started learning about Reliability Centered Maintenance at RIT, I was intrigued to learn that when it comes to hydraulics there are two types of hydraulic systems: the first is clean, efficient, and reliable; the second is dirty, inefficient, and unreliable. I had been working for years on the second type of system, having never seen the clean, efficient, and reliable type. Of course, most of us know that there are several types of hydraulic systems. The point our reliability engineering instructor was trying to make was the importance of cleanliness in terms of hydraulic system reliability and efficiency.

If you were working on a hydraulic system, everyone in the break room knew it the minute you walked through the door. If it wasn't the stink, it was the attitude.

Let's first examine the type of hydraulic system I see most often at manufacturing facilities around the world: the dirty, inefficient, and unreliable. I think in most cases it would be safe to say that on the day this system was delivered and installed, it was most likely clean. I'm sure many parts of the system were freshly painted, the hoses and fittings were dry, and if the engineers who designed the system were optimistic, there is a small possibility the system didn't even include a drip pan!

In the world of manufacturing we are excited to get new equipment. New equipment brings with it the potential to increase business, and we are all thrilled to see our fresh asset start bringing in cash for the business. We can't wait to see how the new toy runs, so we page through the OEM and add the correct amount and type of hydraulic fluid right from the manufacturer's drum—and it may have been at this very moment that we destined our new, clean system to become a dirty, inefficient, and unreliable system.

We put new hydraulic fluid into our system without ever checking to ensure that the fluid we took from the drum met the standard of cleanliness we need to ensure our new hydraulic system is a clean, efficient, and reliable one. What few people understand when it comes to hydraulic systems is that particles as small as 2 microns can have a significant effect on the performance of hydraulic components and pump life. As we look at hydraulic systems today, more than 80% of hydraulic system failures are directly related to the contamination or cleanliness of the hydraulic fluid.

Hydraulic leaks like the one pictured above are a common occurrence with dirty, unreliable, and inefficient hydraulic systems. It is important to understand that while the system is under pressure and warm, the fluid leaks out. When it is shut down and cools, the dirt collected around the leak site will be sucked into your system and result in abrasive wear of the components.

When it comes to hydraulic systems, dirt is the enemy. The contamination of our hydraulic fluid leads to a large list of failure modes that soon define the unreliable, inefficient future of your asset. Contaminants within the fluid cause more wear to your pump, and wear of the pump creates more contaminants within the fluid. Particles in the 3–20 micron range pass freely through standard filtration systems, resulting in erosion and abrasion of servo valves and ports. This abrasion now compounds the amount of increased wear particles in this closed-loop system, and soon the servo valves will begin to stick open, and fluid will continuously bypass and heat up. Servo valves that stay closed result in increased system pressure, and as pressure increases so does temperature. Relief valves will lift and fluid will bypass to the reservoir. As the fluid temperature increases, its ability to lubricate is impacted, servos slam open and closed, hoses and fittings begin to leak, and your once new and clean hydraulic system is now in critical condition. While the system is under pressure, fluid weeps from hose connections and fittings. To help keep our work area safe and clean, we install a custom drip pan and add some absorbent pads or pigs to soak up the leaking fluid. We can see dirt collecting around the leaks, so our system has now achieved the status of being both dirty and unreliable—inefficient is about to be added to the mix.

The leaks and servo failures have gotten to a point where we have additional tasks. The first is a daily task to check the reservoir level and add more fluid; the second comes in weekly or monthly filter changes. We shut down on a regular basis now for unscheduled failures, and as the system has a chance to cool, parts of the system that were once warm and under pressure and leaking are now cool under vacuum and sucking more dirt—and worse yet, water—back into the system. The dirt being sucked in at leak points is much larger than the wear particles we discussed before, so the number of failures will increase, as will the temperature of our fluid. At this point we falsely determine that our once clean, reliable, and efficient hydraulic system was not properly designed.

We decide that our system is in need of a redesign. We can't maintain the system temperature the hydraulic fluid needs to be cooled at! The redesign is a fin-fan or water cooler. Congratulations, you are now scraping toast! ("Scraping toast" also comes from one of my RIT instructors, who taught the importance of failure modes by using a toaster as an example. Suppose the timer knob on your toaster were to break and now every time you want toast, the toast pops up black and burnt.) It is here that we discover the difference between a mechanic and an engineer. The former addresses the failure mode and replaces the failed component; the latter designs and installs a toast scraper!

With our new hydraulic fluid cooler, we now have a hydraulic system that is dirty, unreliable, and—thanks to all the leaks, pigs, and oil coolers—also tremendously inefficient. It's time to add a new task: The drip pans have overflowed again, so we need to have a PM to change the pads and pigs twice a week. Don't forget to label the drum full of saturated absorbent pads and pigs as hazardous waste!

(By the way, my favorite anecdote when it comes to pigs and absorbent pads comes from a man who shall remain nameless and a company that should have higher standards for its engineers. As I shared the above story, he was proud to raise his hand and tell me that his company had a system just like the one I had described but that he had found a way to save money: "We squeeze the oil out of them pads and pigs and reuse it!")

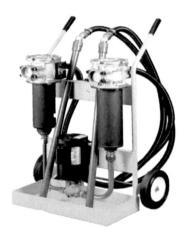

A hydraulic oil filter cart like the one above is critical in removing abrasive particles found even in the brand-new unit you purchased from your supplier. Maintaining a reliable, clean, and efficient hydraulic system requires hydraulic fluid cleaned to the ISO cleanliness standard.

The saddest part of the above story is that I see this everywhere. Dirty, unreliable, and inefficient. How can one not see the added costs that come with operating a system like this? Dirty, unreliable, and inefficient hydraulic systems all result in the following unnecessary costs:

1. The cost of failed parts

2. The cost of maintenance labor

3. The cost of wasted hydraulic fluid

4. The cost of drip pans

5. The cost of pigs and absorbent pads

6. The cost of unnecessary redesigns

7. The cost of extra spare parts we need because our system fails so often

8. The cost of hazardous waste disposal

9. The cost of running cooling fans or coils

10. The cost of unnecessary PMs

11. To cost of downtime in a sold-out market

12. The cost of running at a reduced rate with a overheated system

The question now becomes, "How do we turn this ship around?"

The answer begins with education. We need to begin by training our people to understand the difference between dirty, unreliable, and inefficient hydraulic systems and clean, reliable, and efficient systems. The latter begins with cleanliness. A clean hydraulic system sets the groundwork for achieving a reliable and efficient system.

ISO Standards for Hydraulic Cleanliness

In most companies, this is where the confusion begins. The original equipment manufacturer (OEM) recommends a specific brand of hydraulic fluid. The cleanliness of this fluid should be based on the system operating pressure, temperature, and—most important—the tolerance between metal-to-metal surfaces of your system components. It is your job to ensure the fluid within the system meets or exceeds these requirements at all times.

Operating Pressure →	<1,500 psi	1,500-2,500 psi	>2,500 psi
Servo Valve	16/14/12	15/13/11	14/12/10
Proportional Valve	17/15/12	16/14/12	15/13/11
Variable Volume Pump	17/16/13	17/15/12	16/14/12
Cartridge Valve	18/16/14	17/16/13	17/15/12
Fixed Piston Pump	18/16/14	17/16/13	17/15/12
Vane Pump	19/17/14	18/16/14	17/16/13
Pressure/Flow Control Valve	19/17/14	18/16/14	17/16/13
Solenoid Valve	19/17/14	18/16/14	18/16/14
Gear Pump	19/17/14	18/16/14	18/16/14

Adjust to cleaner levels for duty cycle severity, machine criticality, fluid type (water base) and safety concerns.

Typical Cleanliness Recommendations

The table above lists the cleanliness recommendations for various components in a typical hydraulic system. The level of cleanliness that we need to maintain within our system is dependent on the tightest tolerance and the pressure at which we operate this system. Should we indeed have servo valves and operate the system at greater than 2,500 psi, we need to maintain an ISO cleanliness standard of 14/12/10 at all times.

The ISO Cleanliness Code, ISO 4406:1987, is the perhaps the most widely used international standard for representing the contamination level of industrial fluid power systems. Under ISO 4406, cleanliness is classified by a two- or three-number code, e.g. 16/13, based on the number of particles greater than 5 µm and 15 µm for a two-number standard and respectively in a known volume of fluid. For a three-number ISO standard, we are looking at particles greater than 2 µm, 5 µm, and 15 µm.

Using the following table, we can see a cleanliness rating of 14/12/10 would mean that there were:

- 80 to 160 particles greater than 2 microns in size,

- 20 to 40 particles greater than 5 microns, and

- 5 to 10 particles greater than 15 microns.

The full table of ranges for ISO 4406 is shown below:

Range Number	Number of Particles per ml	
	More than	Up to and Including
24	80 000	160 000
23	40 000	80 000
22	20 000	40 000
21	10 000	20 000
20	5 000	10 000
19	2 500	5 000
18	1 300	2 500
17	640	1 300
16	320	640
15	160	320
14	80	160
13	40	80
12	20	40
11	10	20
10	5	10
9	2.5	5
8	1.3	2.5
7	0.64	1.3
6	0.32	0.64

Now that we know the cleanliness we need to achieve for our fluid, let's discuss how we plan to maintain that standard.

Keeping Your System Clean

Keeping your system clean begins with a filter cart and the education of your lubrication technician. Every ounce of fluid we put into our hydraulic system reservoir needs to be filtered to a cleanliness that meets or exceeds the ISO standard we set for our system. It should also be noted that just because we purchase a drum of new hydraulic fluid does not mean that the fluid in the drum will meet our standard. There are several things that could cause a new drum of hydraulic fluid to fail our cleanliness standard:

• Was the drum really a new drum, and was it cleaned before it was filled? Oil drums do get recycled, and mistakes in the cleaning and filling process do occur.

- Were the drums stored outside at any time? Drums that have been outside collect moisture inside and out; moisture results in corrosion and rust that could contaminate your new drum of oil.

- Has water collected on top of the drum? If the drum has been outside or transported on the back of a truck ,and if water collected on top of the drum, there is a good chance that some of it has also contaminated the fluid.

- Are your drums stored in a cool, dry, temperature-controlled environment? Changes in temperature and humidity result in condensation within the drum, and this little bit of moisture will contaminate your fluid.

- Are the tops of your drums and lubrication room kept clean? Dirt, dust, rust, and other solids contaminate the fluid as drum bungs are removed and pumps are installed.

- Are you topping off fluid levels in the field? Contaminants often enter the system through contaminated top-off containers or from debris around the top-off fittings.

Always add fluid to the hydraulic reservoir through a filter cart with quick-connect fittings to help reduce the probability of contaminants. Use high-performance fluids. Now that we have clean fluid in our reservoir, we must institute a PdM task to perform testing of the fluid on a regular basis.

I would offer the following when it comes to good maintenance practices for your hydraulic systems:

- Start using top-quality high-capacity filters, rerun your requirement calculations, and make sure you have enough filtration so that filters are not being bypassed.

- As stated above, use premium-quality hydraulic fluid.

- Set up fluid analysis on a monthly basis.

- Make sure you are using a filter cart when adding oil to your system, and use the cart to clean the system up should particle counts exceed your ISO standard.

- Use 3 to 5 micron desiccant breathers.

- Set up a good procedure for fluid sampling and testing that ensures the fluid tested is representative of what is in the reservoir.

- Repair all leaks as soon as possible. Remember that leaks will contaminate your system.

- Replace filters based on differential pressure.

- Inspect cylinders for damaged seals and shafts. Schedule a rebuild when noted.

- Set up a good alarm package for your system within your PLC. Alarms should be set to provide a warning that allows for good maintenance: a rise in temperature, pressure, or differential pressure.

Hydraulic System Efficiency

When it comes to hydraulic systems, there seems to be a basic system or package that companies like to purchase. Once they have a system that provides energy to a process, it's at this time that we often begin to take efficiency into consideration. So what is efficiency when it comes to hydraulic systems?

Being efficient when it comes to hydraulic systems, in my mind, is being able to provide adequate hydraulic pressure and flow to operate our field devices in a way that uses the least amount of power with no health safety or environmental impact. If you want an efficient hydraulic system, keep it clean. Keeping your fluid and system clean works not only for reliability but for efficiency as well. Clean systems use less energy, and because they are leak-free there is no safety or environmental impact

On an interesting note, we performed an RCM analysis a year or so ago for a diesel engine facility in Ohio, and we covered a hydraulic system as part of the analysis. While they were having some reliability and cleanliness issues in regard to this system, they did enlighten me to a technique they had put into place to lower the temperature of the hydraulic systems (they had nearly 100 systems within this facility). They had been having high temperature alarms going off on hydraulic systems throughout the plant, and in an attempt to troubleshoot the causes, their thermographer tried using IR imaging to determine if several of the high temperature alarms were real. Attempts to get accurate images of the stainless steel hydraulic piping with the IR camera proved to be futile because of the reflectivity of the stainless. Remembering some information from their IR level 1 class, they decided to paint a section of the stainless pipes white, and in doing so they recognized a 4°F difference between the painted section and unpainted section. They then made the decision to paint all the pipes in the entire system—and with this complete, they realized a 10°F reduction. This not only took the system out of alarm status but it was also enough to shut down the electric fin-fan coolers on most systems.

Reference Notes:

1. Leonard Badal, John Whigham, and Trigg Minnick, "The Importance of ISO Cleanliness Codes," *Machinery Lubrication*, September 2005, http://machinerylubrication.com/article_detail.asp?articleid=800.

2. http://www.equipment.org.

3. Deborah Hayes, DMAX InfraMation 2008 proceedings.

Chapter 9

Electrical Power Distribution

The presence of electrical distribution, or electricity, in industry has been around since the late 1800s. We are grateful for the work that was accomplished by the likes of Thomas Edison, Nikola Tesla, George Westinghouse, and Almarian Decker, to name a few. Today we rely on electricity like never before. Typical industrial electrical systems comprise transformers, distribution systems, switchgears, control panels, lighting, and motors. Not only has our plant equipment become more sensitive with the introduction of so many electronic controllers, but companies also have become more sensitive to loss production, which greatly impacts their profitability. Have you ever stopped to think how important electricity has become in our daily lives? Most of us rarely take the time to evaluate what life would be like without electricity. However, like air and water, we tend to take electricity for granted. I would venture to say that few days pass during which we are not using electricity to do countless functions for us. These functions include lighting, heating, and cooling our homes; powering our entertainment systems and computers; and making our workplace possible. Electricity has become a controllable and convenient form of energy used for an abundance of applications, whether in our homes or in our workplaces.

Have you ever stopped to think how important electricity has become in our daily lives?

Most of the electrical energy consumed in buildings is accounted for by motor-driven systems. By systems, we mean that motors are used for operating equipment such as the plant's HVAC system, pumps, elevators, and fans. Since we have an entire chapter of this book dedicated to motors, in this chapter we will focus primarily on the impact power quality can have on the overall efficiency and reliability of our plants. It should be noted that while electricity typically accounts for 30–40% of industrial energy consumption, it easily accounts for 60–75% of the total utility costs. Other typical energy sources include natural gas, diesel oil, and gasoline. Because of the large percentage of energy cost accounted for by electricity, it is imperative to pay special attention to the electrical-consuming equipment and systems within the facility. It is no secret that electrical energy and costs are saved by managing demand loads, optimizing equipment run hours, improving equipment efficiencies, and maintaining the backbone of the electrical distribution system.

Utilities all around the world have for decades worked extensively to improve what is known as power quality. In fact, the term "power quality" has been around for quite some time. Possibly the oldest mention of power quality was in a paper published in 1968, which detailed a study by the U.S. Navy regarding the specifications for the power required by electronic equipment. *(Ref. 1)* As mentioned previously, it comes as no surprise that our equipment that is commonly controlled by an array of electronic devices requires reliable power. Voltage and current disturbances wreak havoc on our industrial equipment. In 1991, an article appeared in the journal *Business Week* that triggered a great interest in power quality. Within this article, Jane Clemmensen of EPRI was cited as estimating that "power-related problems cost U.S. companies $26 billion a year in lost time and revenue." *(Ref. 2)* So, not only does electricity in most cases account for up to 75% of industrial utility costs, but also power-related failures or problems have the potential to amount to a massive profitability loss.

What is meant by power-related problems and, more important, how can such problems be detected, avoided, and prevented so as to minimize their impact on our bottom line? These questions have certainly been asked by many during the evaluation of such systems, especially when companies are developing and implementing maintenance strategies. How many times have you been involved with an RCM analysis, Failure Mode Analysis, or Root Cause Analysis where often, because of its presence, the electrical system/power/device is called out as a bad actor? Well, if it happened once, it has occurred a thousand times. And to be honest, in most cases, it is a valid judgment. One problem is that so often we are unable to verify because power quality related issues can occur in a blink of an eye and then vanish just as quickly as they occurred. Unless our systems are set up to monitor for such power variations or events, we often are left scratching our heads and wondering what exactly happened and how we can prevent it from occurring again. Just to give you an idea, the following table indicates how IEEE Std.

1159-1995 defines certain voltage magnitude events. An event that would be classified as an overvoltage transient occurs in less than ½ a cycle (60 Hz) or in less than 8 milliseconds. The point is, if we are not monitoring for such events on our critical systems, we likely will not be able to identify the specific reason for such a failure.

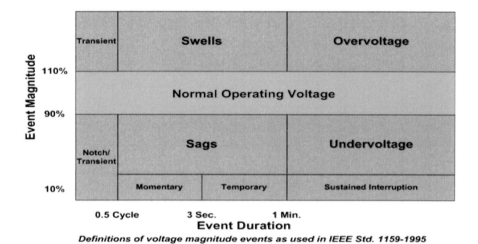

Definitions of voltage magnitude events as used in IEEE Std. 1159-1995

Let's examine seven power quality phenomena and highlight the possible causes and consequences of each:

1. **Voltage Unbalance:** A voltage variation, or unbalance, in a three-phase system can be described as the three voltage magnitudes or phase-angle differences not being equal. There could potentially be a number of possible causes for voltage unbalance; however, the most likely culprits are large single-phase loads (i.e., induction furnaces, traction loads) or the incorrect distribution of all single-phase loads by the three phases of the electrical distribution system. Voltage unbalance can also be the result of capacitor bank anomalies such as a blown fuse on one phase of a three-phase bank. Unbalanced systems imply the existence of a negative sequence that can be harmful to all three-phase loads, resulting in overheating of equipment. The most affected loads are three-phase induction motors. ANSI Std. C84.1-1989 recommends that the maximum voltage unbalance measured at the service entrance under no-load conditions be no greater than 3%. Unbalances greater than 3% can result in significant motor heating and failure if there are not unbalance protection circuits to protect the motor.

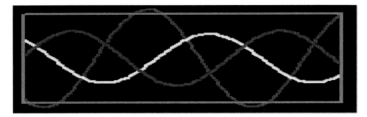

Example of Unbalanced Waveform

2. **Voltage Fluctuation:** This is typically described as an oscillation of voltage value or the amplitude modulated by a signal with a frequency of 0–30 Hz. When the supply voltage magnitude varies, the power flow to equipment will generally vary as well. If voltage variations or fluctuations are large enough or in a certain critical frequency range, the performance of the equipment may be affected. It is rare that voltage variation will affect load behavior; however, one example many have experienced is that of the lighting load (i.e., light flicker). Possible causes of voltage fluctuation are arc furnaces, frequent starting/stopping of motors (i.e., elevators), or other large oscillating loads. Most consequences are common to undervoltages, the most noticeable of which was mentioned earlier: a flickering of light and screens, giving the impression of unsteadiness of visual perception.

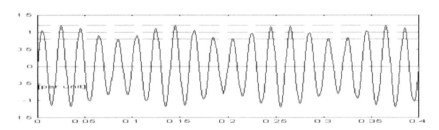

Example of Voltage Fluctuation Waveform

3. **Harmonic Distortion:** This phenomenon can be described as voltage or current waveforms that assume non-sinusoidal waveshapes. In AC electrical power distribution systems, harmonics pertain to any additional frequencies present in the nominal waveshape that are multiples of the fundamental power frequency (i.e., 50 Hz or 60 Hz). There are many possible causes of such distortion. Traditionally, sources included electric machines working above the magnetic saturation level, arc furnaces, welding equipment, rectifiers, and DC brush motors. In the more recent atmosphere, sources

include all non-linear loads such as power electronic equipment, adjustable frequency drives, switched power mode supplies, data processing equipment, and high frequency lighting. When such equipment is installed without the proper design work to include filtering and fine-tuning to balance the subsequent loads, the consequences can be significant. Such consequences include an increased likelihood of resonance; neutral overload in three-phase systems; and overheating of equipment such as transformers, capacitors, motors, and power supplies for emergency lighting. In some cases, such harmonic frequencies can cause large harmonic currents and unusually high voltages. The large currents can overload some portion of the circuit, resulting in circuit breaker trips and blown fuses. These high voltages can cause insulation breakdown and equipment failures. Other consequences include electromagnetic interference with communication systems, errors in measures when using average multimeters, and nuisance tripping of thermal protection devices.

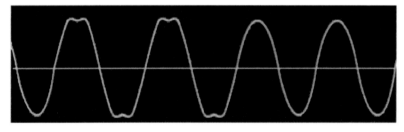

Example of Harmonic Distortion Waveform

4. **High Frequency Variations:** Also known as notches or noise, high frequency variations can be described as a superimposing of high frequency signals on the waveform of the power system frequency. Possible causes of such variations include electromagnetic interferences provoked by Hertzian waves such as microwaves, television diffusion, and radiation due to welding machines, arc furnaces, and some electronic equipment. Improper system grounding has also been known to cause high frequency variations. Possible consequences of this phenomenon include disturbances on sensitive electronic equipment, which usually is not destructive. However, there are known instances of data loss and data processing errors when information technology systems are affected.

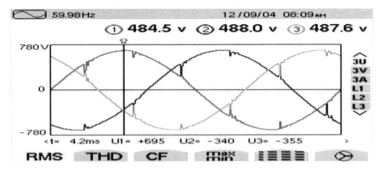

Example of High Frequency Variation Waveform

5. **Undervoltages:** Also known as dips or sags, undervoltages can be described as a decrease of the normal voltage level between 10–90% of the nominal rms voltage, for durations of zero to five cycles up to one minute. Voltage sags are mostly caused by short-circuit faults in the system, such as on the transmission or distribution lines. Voltage sags are also known to result from overloads and the starting of large motors. The interest in voltage sags is mainly due to the problems they cause on several types of equipment such as adjustable speed drives, process control equipment (i.e., PLCs), and computers. These particular assets are notorious for their sensitivity and in some cases may lead to a process stoppage when the rms voltage drops below 90% for longer than one or two cycles.

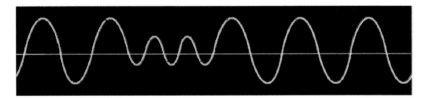

Example of Undervoltage Waveform

6. **Overvoltages:** The common power quality phenomenon referred to as overvoltages, also known as swells, can be described as a momentary increase of the voltage at the power frequency, with the duration between one cycle and typically less than one minute. Some possible causes of overvoltage include excessive starting/stopping of large loads, badly dimensioned power sources, and badly regulated transformers (typically during off-peak hours). The possible consequences can have a wide range of severity, from data loss and flickering of lighting, to stoppage or damage of sensitive electronic

equipment, to the destruction of power system equipment. In fact, one such instance that I had the opportunity to examine and troubleshoot related to a long duration overvoltage, which was caused by a resonance between the nonlinear magnetizing reactance of a transformer and a capacitance. Such an event is often referred to as ferroresonance. In this particular instance, it was found that utility capacitor bank switching events triggered the presence of ferroresonance, which was observed at a pad mounted 500KVA, 12,470V to 480/277V transformer. Upon further investigation of the transformer, it was found that the individual laminations of the top yoke of the core were shorted together. Use of infrared thermography (see below) indicated a hot spot with a delta T rise of 328°F. The shorted laminations had created a circulating current in the core that generated heat and increased the losses (watts) and costs associated with operating the transformer. Close visual inspection of the hot spot area showed signs of localized heating (flaking varnish, oxidation, reddish color) and damaged core laminations (bent, dented, punched, scratched), especially along the edge of the laminations. A cost benefit analysis based on the age of the transformer (30+ years) and usable service life indicated it was cost prohibitive to repair the transformer; therefore a new transformer was purchased as a replacement. Further study and design of the overvoltages led to the installation of capacitor bank controls and surge arresters.

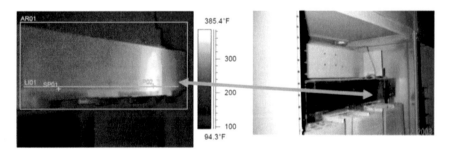

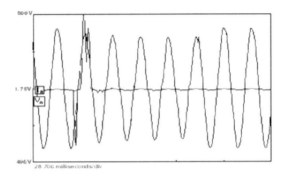

Example of Undervoltage Waveform

7. **Transient Overvoltages:** This is the last common power quality phenomenon we will discuss. Transient overvoltages, also known as spikes, can be described as very fast variations of the voltage value for durations of several microseconds to a few milliseconds. These spikes are known to reach extremely high levels. This phenomenon is very similar to the previously discussed overvoltage, with the difference being the time duration and the high level of voltage. As with overvoltages, possible causes can range from the switching of lines or power factor correction capacitors to the disconnection of large loads. Another typical culprit of (high frequency) transient overvoltages is Mother Nature and the natural occurrence of lightning. The possible consequences also are very similar to those of overvoltages in that transients can have a wide range of severity, from data loss or flickering of lighting, to stoppage or damage of sensitive electronic equipment, to the destruction of power system equipment. Transients are also known to cause electromagnetic interference. Surge suppressors are often used to protect and absorb the energy in high frequency transients. These suppressors are devices that conduct across the power line when some voltage threshold is exceeded. However, the resulting high frequency current pulses can still create problems for sensitive electronic systems, especially delicate instrumentation. Extremely fast transients (EFTs) have rise and fall times in the nanosecond region. Such EFTs are caused by arcing faults, which can be found in bad brushes of motors. Standard line filters, included on almost all electronic equipment, remove these dangerous EFTs.

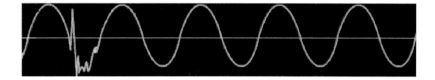

Example of Undervoltage Waveform

So, at this point you are probably wondering how all these power quality issues relate to being energy efficient. It is critical to realize that each of the seven discussed phenomena at some level, if left to their own devices, will degrade industrial equipment, whether large electrical transmission devices, motors, or electronics. When equipment is degraded, results typically are seen in the form of losses in performance (small variances as well as large) and electrical power losses.

For totally resistive loads, electrical power is the product of voltage and current used.

$$Power = Voltage * Current$$

The basic unit of power is watts (W) and is normally measured in kilowatts (kW), which is 1,000 watts. Electrical energy is the power that is used over time and thus is a product of power and time.

$$Electrical\ Energy = Power * Time$$

In circuits that have inductive elements such as motor windings, transformer windings, and lamp ballasts, there are two components of power. One is the actual power absorbed, or used, by the component to perform the desired work (i.e., step up or down voltage, move an object, or light an element). Actual power is also referred to as real power or active power. The other component of power is apparent power, used for magnetizing the magnetic elements.

Power factor is the ratio of active power to apparent power. Often, utility companies penalize consumers if the overall power factor is below a certain value. Power factors range from zero to one. The highest power factor of 1.0 is achieved if there is no reactive power, which would be the case for a totally resistive load.

$$Power\ Factor = \cos \theta = active\ power\ (kW)\ /\ apparent\ power\ (kVA)$$

Electricity charges paid to utility companies can be lowered by reducing electrical energy usage, maximizing power demand, and improving the overall power factor.

Recall the transformer case from above that was found to have internal core damage, causing mounting power (W) losses. These losses were going unnoticed by the owner, and not only were they paying for the losses in energy usage but they were also impacted by the ancillary damage and subsequent losses.

Transformers are generally efficient and have low energy losses. The losses are normally around 1–2% of transformer capacity and depend upon transformer type and size. Transformer losses are mainly due to copper losses, eddy current losses, and hysteresis losses. Such transformer losses can also be categorized into core losses (no-load losses) and coil losses (load losses). Load losses are the copper losses, which are due to power dissipation in the form of heat caused by resistance of the conductor. No-load losses are eddy current and hysteresis losses, which are due to the magnetizing current used to energize the core of the transformer. These no-load losses are typically passed through the core, whether in magnetic form or through random currents, dissipating power in the form of heat.

In typical plant power design, transformers are sized based on the expected demand, which far exceeds actual load. Since no-load loss is a function of the kVA capacitance of the transformer and continues as long as the transformer is energized, it is extremely important if energy efficiency is your desire to select transformers that better match the actual load requirements. Now, you are likely going to say the same thing I always did: "We need to design for growth because that is exactly what always ends up happening and we want to be prepared." In such situations where transformer capacity exceeds the demand and the transformers are already selected and installed, it may be beneficial to transfer loads and de-energize some transformers to minimize no-load losses. Manufacturers estimate the no-load losses for transformers over 500 kVA to be about 0.3% of the rated capacity.

Example of Savings by De-Energizing Transformer

Let's assume a plant uses five transformers, each of which is 1,000 kVA. If the maximum total plant load is measured to be 3,750 kVA, estimate the electrical energy savings in dollars that can be achieved if one of the 1,000 kVA transformers is de-energized. Assume the average power factor to be 0.9, while using the average industrial retail price in June 2009 of 7.18 cents per kWh.

Solution: If the no-load losses are taken to be 0.3%, the savings by de-energizing the 1,000 kVA transformer equals:

no-load kVA losses * power factor * operating hours

$$= (1000 * 0.3\%) * 0.9 * 8760 = 23,652 \text{ kWh/year}$$

$$= 23,652 * \$0.0718$$

$$= \$1,698.21 \text{ per year}$$

Granted, we are not doing the full cost benefit analysis as we would have to account for load shifting costs, but this is certainly an area of evaluation that should be considered.

Two other areas of concern to plant electrical distribution opportunities include understanding the ability to load shed and lighting applications. Both of these areas are subjects that could easily be an entire chapter (or, in some cases, a full book) of their own, but we will briefly mention them here. Load shedding can be as simple as in the example with the transformer above, which requires an understanding of both the total capacity and maximum requirement of the equipment. Or, in another example, it could represent the ability to shut down certain equipment, such as chillers, based upon run-time requirements (i.e., nights and weekends).

Lighting applications and the potential cost savings opportunities can be dramatic. In fact, electricity used to operate lighting systems represents a significant portion of total electricity consumed in the United States, where they consume approximately 20% of the electricity generated. *(Ref. 3)*

Choices for lighting sources, fixtures, bulbs, etc., are numerous; depending on the intent of the area and the design of the building, certain choices are better than others. However, when it comes to improving lighting efficiency, there are three basic steps to follow. First, identify necessary light quantity and quality to perform visual tasks. Next, increase light source efficiency if occupancy is frequent. Last, optimize lighting controls if occupancy is infrequent. I have taken this three-step process into my own home and seen dramatic cost savings. Granted, I have three kids who love to turn on every light in the house, but I have replaced where applicable all standard light bulbs with the compact fluorescent lamps and have installed multiple occupancy sensors around the home. On average since the replacements, I have seen a monthly cost savings of roughly 22%. I have seen similar numbers within the industrial environments that range from as low as 20% energy savings in offices, to 45% savings in plant floor workspace, to 70% savings in warehouses.

Reference Notes:

1. H.H. Kajihara, "Quality Power for Electronics," *Electro-Technology*, vol. 82, n. 5, November 1968, p. 46.

2. R.D. Hof, "The 'Dirty Power' Clogging Industry's Pipeline," *Business Week,* April 8, 1991.

3. E. Mills and M. Piette, 1993, "Advanced Energy-Efficient Lighting Systems: Progress and Potential," *Energy: The International Journal*, vol. 18, p. 75.

Other Sources:

Allied Reliability Inc., *PM/PdM Electrical Best Practices*.

Department of Energy, http://www1.eere.energy.gov/buildings/.

Steve Doty and Wayne C. Turner, *Energy Management Handbook*, Fairmont Press, 2009, 7th ed.

Chapter 10

Steam and Condensate

L et me begin with saying that this chapter had the possibility, like no other, to be huge and overdone. When I began doing research I had a hundred pages of information and was still looking up information on the web! I needed to make a decision about clear boundaries on this topic, or the next thing you know we would be discussing the most efficient way to tune the fuel efficiency of your boiler—a topic way beyond my level of expertise. I decided to think back to the title of the book, *Clean, Green, and Reliable*, stick to that theme, and explain how reliable steam and condensate systems are more energy efficient. Plus, I will offer some simple operating and maintenance tasks that we can do to maintain reliable and efficient steam and condensate systems.

From turning turbines to heating our buildings for comfort, steam is often the choice because it is relatively simple to produce.

Reliable and Efficient Steam

In the world of manufacturing, we use steam for an unlimited number of uses. From turning turbines to create steam, to heating our buildings for comfort, steam is often the choice because it is relatively simple to produce and can be a somewhat reliable source of energy. If the words "relatively simple" and "somewhat reliable" seem cautious, it's because many of us tend to take steam for granted. There seems to be a mentality that concludes, "We have steam readily available in the area for use in our process, so why not take advantage of it being there and use it as many things as possible?"

This is where the trouble begins. Let's hope that in designing the steam header for your process equipment, your engineers performed the proper calculations for the steam and condensate loop, including those for temperature, pressure, density, volume, heat, work, and energy. This ensures that we have the right amount of steam and energy available for manufacturing. Any additions to this system that demand steam will now affect this system and may have an impact on its original intent. While this all would seem to be common sense, those of us who have worked with manufacturing companies around the world can share stories of unreliable and inefficient steam systems.

On a recent tour of a manufacturing facility in the United States, I was distracted by the number of steam traps that were discharging to the open air. Standing in one place for less than two minutes, I counted 20 traps of various types openly discharging. So I asked my guide, "Why are you discharging your condensate this way?"

He replied, "We kept having trouble with the traps and the condensate system. Traps were sticking open or freezing, creating havoc with our process. So in order to save money and make the problem more evident, we disconnected the discharge to our traps. Now if one is blowing through we can see it."

I then asked, "If your traps are blowing through like the four I can see right now, do you do anything about it?"

He replied, "Steam is cheap, so the traps don't rank too high on the work order backlog list."

That evening I did a little research in the hotel room, and the next day I provided him with the following information:

"In a system of 1,000 steam traps, it is assumed that the average orifice size of a blow-through is estimated at 1/16 inch, the average pressure is 150 psig, and the cost of steam production is $4.00/1,000 lbs. It is also assumed that the plant steam is in operation 365 days/year, 24 hours/day. Based on these assumptions, the steam loss per day is 453 lbs. per trap at a cost of $1.81/day/trap or $662.25/year loss per trap. A conservative assumption that only 10% of the traps are faulty would result in an annual cost of $66,225 in lost steam within the system."

Also consider that they were discharging the condensate to the atmosphere instead of returning it for recovery. So for each trap that was discharging condensate to the atmosphere, we now have to make that up with fresh water that will need to be preheated and treated at additional costs.

The sad fact is, the above example is closer to being the norm rather than the exception. Because I provide reliability consulting services at manufacturing sites around the world, it is far more common for me to see unreliable and inefficient steam systems than it is to see reliable and efficient systems.

Common Mistakes in Steam Systems—and Suggested Solutions

1. **Undersized in Design:** There are a number of excuses when it comes to a system being under-designed. The end result is a system that is abused and inefficient. Evidence of an under-designed system includes poor manufacturing process control, process upsets, systems that freeze, and water hammer. You will need to walk your system down and account for all the areas using steam off your supply header and perform usage and load calculations. The Department of Energy Industrial Technologies Program has an extensive collection of technical resources available to help facilities improve their industrial energy system efficiency. Fact sheets, tip sheets, optimization software, case studies, workshops, and more are available at no cost through the ITP website.

2. **Improper Installation:** This failure mode usually goes hand in hand with improper or undersized design. The end result is an inefficient steam supply. I want all plant managers to understand one thing about installing a steam header and supply feeds: When it comes to quality work, there are two types of tradespeople—those who are trained and certified and those who are not. If your tradespeople have not been trained and certified on how to properly install a steam and condensate system, you are taking a huge risk. Given time, they will make changes that will screw the entire system up. Evidence of improperly installed steam systems include lots of missing or temporary covering or insulation; mixing of metals; poor supports; poor pitch, no pitch, or incorrect pitch; improper placement or use of valves; lots of leaks; system freezes; and traps that discharge to the atmosphere.

3. **Improper Insulation:** This might be the most common form of waste when it comes to inefficient steam systems. Improper insulation leads to heat losses that further tax your steam supply. Although this loss is rarely calculated, there is visual evidence in damaged, missing, and temporary insulation. The real issue is how much heat are we losing and what is the cost? The calculation here is difficult. How much pipe is exposed, how much is poorly insulated, and how much insulation is damaged? The solution comes down to making some simple decisions based on safety, reliability, and energy efficiency. How many of your

people have been burned by being exposed to steam piping or steam leaks? How many people have been cut by improperly installed or damaged insulation covering? The pipe covering for your steam piping is there for two specific reasons: to minimize heat loss and to protect your employees. Reliable and efficient steam systems are well insulated and the insulation is well maintained. It is of extreme importance that you budget money to maintain your steam piping insulation each year.

4. **Poor Steam Quality:** When we think of steam, good steam quality means we have steam available at the point of use in the correct amount, pressure, and temperature; the steam is free of incondensable gasses; the steam is clean (free of rust, dirt, or other solids); and the steam is dry. I have to confess that in the time I worked as a maintenance mechanic I had little to no understanding of steam quality and its effects on the reliability and efficiency of a steam system. Evidence of poor quality steam includes steam trap failures, high corrosion rates, poor heat transfer, system freezing, and leaks. Steam quality is of extreme importance when it comes to reliability and efficiency; as a result, I will offer some additional details on how to maintain steam quality.

The steam leak pictured above is just one example of the thousands of steam leaks I see at plants around the word. This system is suffering from at least a few of the common mistakes we see with steam and condensate systems. It is quite clearly a victim of improper insulation, as well as improper design. This leak is not only a waste of energy but it sooner or later will result in unscheduled equipment downtime—and is an obvious safety hazard.

•   Purge your steam of air and incondensable gases at start-up and after system maintenance. With a typical steam start-up we turn the steam on, and the piping—which is filled with air (78% nitrogen, 21% oxygen, and 0.03% carbon dioxide)—mixes with the steam, and we now have a mixture that is 75% steam and 25% air. The resulting mixture reduces the pressure and temperature of the steam. This is known as Dalton's Law of Partial Pressures—and if you think Dalton's Law is hogwash, consider the following equation:

A steam/air mixture made up of ¾ steam and ¼ air by volume. The total pressure is 4 bar a. Determine the temperature of the mixture:

$$\frac{3}{4} \times 4 \text{ bar a} = 3 \text{ bar a}$$

Therefore, the steam has an effective pressure of only 3 bar a as opposed to its apparent pressure of 4 bar a. The mixture would have a temperature of only 134°C rather than the expected saturation temperature of 144°C. This phenomenon is not only of importance in heat exchange applications (where the heat transfer rate increases with an increase in temperature difference), but also in process applications, where a minimum temperature may be required to achieve a chemical or physical change in a product or, more important, where the steam temperature is being used in a food application to kill a specific bacteria. *(Ref. 1)*

To address the issue of Dalton's Law we need to train our operations and maintenance personnel to purge air and incondensable gases from the steam supply and develop a procedure to do so.

• Improper water treatment in your boiler feed can result in large amounts of carbon dioxide and oxygen being entrained in the feed water. These entrained gases can corrode the boiler as well as the steam piping system. This corrosion will not only reduce the life of your boiler and steam system but also reveal itself in rust and scale in the boiler and steam piping. The rust and scale will break plugging strainers and traps; if these problems remain unresolved, large amounts of condensate will form in the steam piping and water hammer will result. Remember, two of the objectives of good steam quality are clean and dry—if your steam is not clean, it will be very difficult to keep the steam dry.

Keeping your steam clean comes down to water treatment, water sampling, and strainer maintenance. We need to have a boiler water treatment program in place that minimizes the concentration of dissolved carbon dioxide by dematerializing and degassing feed water prior to the boiler. Steam strainers should be installed upstream of every trap and should be included as part of your steam trap maintenance program.

Keeping your steam dry is essential to reliability and efficiency. Wet steam not only is erosive but also can lead to severe water hammer and damage to your steam piping system. Causes of wet steam include poor insulation, improper water treatment, improper start-up, and trap failures. In severe cases of water hammer, pipe fittings may fracture with an almost explosive effect. The consequence may be the loss of live pressurized steam at the fracture, a serious safety hazard.

Keeping your steam dry is dependent on three things, in my mind: 1) good insulation, 2) reliable and well-maintained traps, and 3) the use of moisture separators that remove moisture droplets allowed into the steam flow. This condensed moisture is then removed from the separator via the steam trap.

If you want more great information on steam and condensate systems, check out the Spirax Sarco website.

Condensate

I have some strong opinions when it comes to condensate systems. Most companies install them because they initially recognize the need and financial value of recovering the condensate and returning this valuable resource to the boiler feed tank. Then we begin to manufacture product, we make lots of money on this product—because this, after all, is why we are in business—and we slowly lose sight of why we have a condensate system.

In more than 15 years of performing Reliability Centered Maintenance analyses for companies around the world, I can remember including only one condensate system in an analysis. Yet in touring plants I commonly see traps discharging to the atmosphere, condensate headers that are leaking or dumping into the industrial sewer, traps installed without strainers, and strainers that are cracked and leaking, showing evidence that they were at some point frozen. Adding to the list of trash just described, we have missing, damaged, or inadequate pipe covering and missing pipe hangers—not to mention, to help thaw what once was a frozen mess, a few coils of rubber steam hose left connected with the valve partly open to ensure the hoses don't freeze as well. Looking at this eyesore and listening to live steam and condensate escaping from the system, I can visualize your company's money blowing away in the wind like leaves in the fall.

I begin with a conversation I have had at least 50 times: "Do you have any idea what all this leakage is costing you?"

"What, this steam and condensate leaking? We've got bigger fish to fry here, Doug. These traps have been a nuisance since Day One, and we just don't have the people it would take to make it right."

While the above example is a dripleg for a steam header, as shown by the IR image it is clearly defective and leaking through steam full time. It's just another example of wasted energy and poor maintenance practices.

"Are you seeing the secondary damage that is being caused by all these leaks?" I ask. "Look at the concrete on this pad here—it's pitted and cracking. Look at all the paint and corrosion on your piping and supports. What is it costing you to maintain your boiler feed water?"

"I really have no idea, Doug. The boiler and utilities are a whole different department."

"Who is supposed to be maintaining this equipment?"

"Well, our utilities maintenance group started out trying to maintain the traps, but we eliminated them about 10 years ago. Now we just replace them as needed."

Finally, I say: "If I were you, I would take a close look at what this entire mess is costing the company. And don't kid yourself—losing this much steam and condensate has a direct effect on your process."

When it comes to condensate systems there are several common mistakes we all seem to make. Most are made because we don't train our people in how the system is supposed to work, and we don't perform the maintenance required to keep it working correctly.

More than 45% of all the fuel burned by U.S. manufacturers is consumed to raise steam. Steam is used to heat raw materials and treat semi-finished products. It is also a power source for equipment, as well as for building heat and electricity generation. Many manufacturing facilities can recapture energy through the installation of more efficient steam equipment and processes. The whole system must be considered to optimize energy and cost savings. *(Ref. 2)*

The primary purpose of an effective condensate recovery system is to make the most effective use of all remaining steam and condensate energy after process use. Key components include condensate return piping, steam traps, flash tanks, and condensate pumps. When it comes to condensate systems, one of the most common mistakes comes from the misunderstanding that the condensate system or piping is a simple drain that returns condensate to the boiler feed tank. Like any other process system at your plant, the condensate return system requires solid engineering and maintenance practices. Mistakes generally begin when we make the assumption that we can add an unlimited number of new traps at various pressures to our existing system, which was engineered for a predetermined flow.

In order to ensure that the condensate piping is adequately sized and can accommodate the additional traps, we need to determine the existing flow as well as the expected new flow. Condensate piping must accommodate two-phase flow B liquid and vapor. The vapor portion of the condensate stream is more voluminous than the liquid portion. In general, condensate piping must be sized to handle the flash and blow-through steam rather than just the liquid portion. Condensate piping that is sized only for the liquid portion will be grossly undersized.

Common Mistakes in Condensate Systems and Suggested Solutions

1. **Inadequate Drainage of Condensate Piping:** Condensate piping must be not only properly sized to accommodate two-phase flow but also pitched to the recovery or boiler feed tank. Inadequate pitch will cause water hammer and create a serious safety concern. In most cases, we installed the initial piping system correctly but then added new branches and traps that were not properly pitched, or over time piping hangers failed or were removed.

    The best way to ensure we steer clear of this issue is to have a Management of Change (MOC) process in place, where all new additions to the system are properly calculated and designed. Annual inspections of piping pitch and support will ensure that existing pitch is maintained.

2. **Steam Trap Failures:** Inoperative or poorly maintained steam traps can result in water hammer. Should the trap fail in an open state, raw steam will be added to the condensate system and could give rise to a serious safety concern.

    I recommend that all steam traps be part of a comprehensive trap maintenance program that includes tagging, routine screener blow-down, and PdM assessment of the trap using ultrasonic listening tools as well as infrared imaging inspections.

3. **Inadequate Training of Operations and Maintenance:** When employees are not trained in how a system operates, they will make their own assumptions along with mistakes that will impact the system operation and, worse, the safety or your plant. Steam and condensate systems incidents occur every year, and the most common cause is inadequate training. Water hammer, the unexpected release and associated shock wave of high-pressure steam/condensate, can cause death, severe injury, and extensive property damage. In one such case, a water hammer filled a confined space with 120 psi steam on June 7, 1993, killing the Hanford site power operator who opened the valve. Although direct cleanup costs totaled only $34,000, the costs necessary to upgrade systems—including inspection, component replacement, procedure revision, labeling, and drawing—and to implement adequate conduct of operations exceeded $5 million. *(Ref. 3)*

    All operations, engineering, and maintenance people who are responsible for the operations and maintenance of process steam piping need to be trained in how the steam and condensate systems work, the process for making changes to these systems (MOC), lock out tag out, as well as proper shutdown and start-up procedures.

4. **Inadequate Insulation:** This may be the most common issue I see in touring plants. We invite our own problems when we maintain these systems by removing the covering and never replacing it, or by doing a poor job of replacing the insulation. Signs of poor insulation include system freezing, condensate leaks, and safety issues such as skin burns. Missing or poorly installed insulation invites water into the insulation, resulting in undercover corrosion and more leaks.

The steam header in the photo above has been damaged and left unrepaired, inviting undercover corrosion. If left open to the elements, the header will experience an accelerated corrosion rate and will eventually leak, resulting in a major loss of steam and the shutdown of at least a portion of this plant.

Good insulation is everyone's job. Missing or damaged insulation on steam and condensate systems should be a safety concern and reported as such. I recommend a twice-annual formal system walk-down inspection of insulation.

Now, if I haven't scared you into understanding that steam and condensate systems require excellence on the part of operations, engineering, and maintenance, let's look at the potential gains that can be made in operating a clean, reliable, and energy-efficient steam and condensate system.

100

The time to stop neglecting and abusing your system is now. Fuel costs are at an all-time high, and manufacturing companies around the world are looking for proven ways to lower their operating costs. Reliability and energy efficiency in your steam and condensate systems promise a number of benefits that lower costs and improve productivity. While I covered some of the higher-level common failure modes of steam and condensate systems, I would strongly recommend performing a RCM Blitz™ analysis of your specific systems to uncover the failure modes unique to your operating context and develop a complete maintenance strategy to ensure both reliability and energy efficiency.

Clean, Reliable, and Efficient Steam and Condensate Systems Will Provide the Following Benefits:

1. Reduction in energy costs for heating boiler makeup water.

2. Reduction in chemical treatment costs for boiler feed water.

3. Energy savings from poorly insulated piping. (An uninsulated section of piping of 4" piping that is 10 feet long will cost twice as much in steam per year than it would to insulate.)

4. Energy savings from repaired steam and condensate leaks.

5. Energy savings from faulty steam traps.

6. Maintenance cost savings from a reduction in emergency or demand maintenance on steam and condensate systems.

7. Increased efficiency and heat transfer for operating equipment.

Reference Notes:

1. Dalton's Law of Partial Pressure, http://www.engineeringtoolbox.com/steam-air-mixture-d_427.html.

2. "Energy Efficiency Impact on Industrial Steam Operations," Alliance to Save Energy, http://ase.org/resources/energy-efficiency-impact-industrial-steam-operations.

3. H.L. Debban and L.E. Eyre, "Condensate Induced Water Hammer in a Steam Distribution System Results in Fatality," Department of Energy, 1996, http://www.osti.gov/bridge/purl.cover.jsp;jsessionid=1C3802D5A1C9 F5485DDDAB303CF2CDF2?purl=/206638-gId7sm/webviewable/.

Chapter 11

Case Studies

Case Study 1: Air Leak Program

Ultrasonic Emissions (UE) leak detection is paying big dividends at one of our clients' plants. The program was initially placed into operation in February 2009 during a winter shutdown. An attempt was made to cover the entire plant in a week. The goal for the week was to send operations and/or instrument maintenance personnel with the leak detection technician in order to fix on the spot all leaks not requiring parts to be ordered.

Before sharing the secrets of saving more than a quarter-million dollars per year in the leak program's first year, we'll provide a little background first.

What Does a Typical Leak Program Look Like?

Typically, an air leak program involves a properly-trained technician taking an instrument into the field and walking down an assigned area seeking to identify air leaks. As the air leaks are located, the leak identification tag is filled out and hung at the leak site. The technician then records location, component involved, repair to be made, and severity of the leak (in decibels) for the work order. The technician will take a picture or two to help the planner and the maintenance technician locate the leak.

Typically, an air leak program involves a properly-trained technician taking an instrument into the field and walking down an assigned area seeking to identify air leaks.

When the work orders get to the planner, he determines what parts must be replaced and what permits will be needed based on accessibility of the component and any safety considerations such as scaffolding, fall protection, and lockout requirements. Once the job is scheduled, the leak is repaired in an average of one to two months after it was located. Once the leak repair work order reaches status 82 (ready for quality check), the technician who identified the leak returns to the field to verify the leak is repaired satisfactorily. The failure rate for air leak quality checks has been 19% over the past year. The failed or missed repairs often require more planning, additional parts, and manpower to complete the task.

The Bigger, the Better

One thing we noticed while performing one of the first surveys at the plant was that there are many more leaks out there that *don't* need to be written up versus ones that do. In other words, once you realize how many leaks there actually are, you can be choosy about the ones you wish to invest time and resources into repairing. In an ultrasonically "quiet" area without steam leaks, the background "noise" level is so low that tiny leaks can be located. These are the ones that would make small bubbles at a slow but steady rate on a fitting without Teflon tape, for example. If I stop to write this one up and others like it, I'll run out of time before getting to that leak toward the end of the route that is 15 times bigger. Although all leaks are important to eliminate, it is vital to set priorities. You do the math! I'd have to find 15 of those little leaks to have the payback that the one large one has.

Having the Right People in the Front of the Parade

When the shutdown was approaching, we had a meeting with the newly appointed energy director "czar" for the plant. He had some ideas about cutting expenses on a bigger scale. He saw the opportunity to locate and repair leaks during the relative quiet of the shutdown and would have us look for leaks over the entire plant during that week. The energy director is a charismatic man who has a contagious energy and enthusiasm for his work. If he had shown the least doubt that we could have accomplished the goal he'd set, we would have certainly raised more than enough objections to doom his plan to failure. We felt inspired to prove it could be done. With enough support from the plant and from site contractors, we could make the difference the director was hoping to achieve: the shutting down of one of the plant's nine compressors.

Teamwork in the Face of Barriers

Right off the starting line we were thrown some real challenges. First, the operations support wasn't going to work out, partly because of the lack of maintenance experience and access to the parts we needed. There was also uncertainty among the team as to how much support we were going to have and just how the logistics of people, parts, and plant configuration would play into our successful execution of this daunting task. Second, we found that some of the contractors didn't have the resources to provide support for leak repairs. So with everything but the energy director's enthusiasm flagging from the start, we split into teams that would cover at least two areas at a time, with the plant repairing the leaks they could, ordering parts for those they could, and having us write up the leaks that needed more than a fitting or a regulator. We covered nearly all the plant and wrote work orders to repair 70–80% of the identified leaks.

Getting a Good Start

The initial idea didn't immediately appear to make practical sense to everyone. We had some folks who would say, "We've tried before with no success." After about five months, an instrument shop technician was dedicated to the leak surveys as they were performed. The first survey in another area of the plant proved this process very successful. Twenty-six leaks were repaired on the spot with 15 more written up for later repair. A total of $15,000/year in savings was identified that day, with almost 2/3 fixed on the spot.

One of the keys to making an air leak program as successful as this one is putting together a support team that is responsible for addressing problems as they are found. Approximately one-third of the located leaks can be repaired on the spot with very few parts. These leaks are generally of the type that involve pinhole leaks in plastic tubing, loose compression fittings, or using Teflon tape on a small pipe fitting at the instrument connection. By repairing leaks on the spot, we see savings begin immediately and eliminate the intermediate time-consuming steps of work order preparation, planning, scheduling, craft repair in the field, and quality checks.

Don't Miss the Unseen Savings

If a leak is identified and can't be fixed on the spot, or if a dedicated escort cannot be supplied, a work order is written, a planner walks the job down and plans it, the job is scheduled, and a technician is assigned the job to complete. The technician will likely walk the job down, complete the Pre-Job Hazard Analysis, and arrange access to the equipment and parts through operations and the warehouse as required. Once the leak is repaired and the work order passes to status 82, the leak identifier will go to the field and perform a quality check to ensure proper repair was made. A breakdown of the resources to complete this work follows:

Write Work Order	¼ hour
Planning	½ hour
Scheduling	3 minutes
Leak Repair	1 hour
Quality Check	½ hour
Total	2.3 man-hours per leak

These are certainly conservative estimates. The 26 leaks that were repaired on the spot in the example above by one instrument technician spending eight man-hours in the field would have cost an additional 59.8 man-hours (26 x 2.3) if they'd been written up instead.

Together this team has identified and repaired leaks over the past year that total a savings of $250,000/year. This does not include $66,000/year from two very large leaks located and repaired early in the program. These two leaks had also challenged the compressed air system's ability to perform its intended function. According to the energy director's quarterly Leak Tag Report of January 2010, the plant has been running at **"75 psi air pressure, with very few events of low pressure in January. We have been able to run with TWO compressors offline for over 3 months now. We have been able to run with 3 compressors offline at times."** So the results are not just being reported on paper but have been manifest in the testimony of the plant's performance... Real savings in dollars and energy savings, and that looks like a successful program.

So what are the secrets? Just do what you've been trained to do and find someone with the enthusiasm and "energy" to spare.

Air Leak Program Report

Across the plant we have tagged 283 leaks that have a value of $878,000. We have repaired 200 of them already (78%) with a value of more than $591,000.

Another notable improvement that we are seeing is in BOD generation. Preliminary results show a 5% reduction in loading this month, and for the first time in 11 months we were under 80,000 lb./day average! After the new year, we started recharging our efforts with mini-campaigns across the plant.

We were averaging about 60–80 leaks per month for the first three months of the program; we are now around 20–30. Below is our rollout schedule for the remainder of the plant.

1. **Prep**   6. **Modhouse**

2. **Boiler**   7. **Elevator**

3. **Feedhouse**   8. **Oil**

4. **Mill Steep**   9. **CSU**

5. **FX**

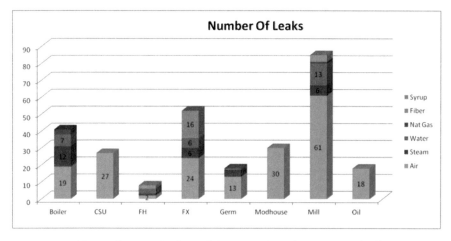

The Feedhouse*, Boiler and FX teams have done a nice job of
identifying leaks in their areas.
*some fiber leaks listed as mill due to equipment assignment in the process area

Allied continues to be the foundation of our leak tag program. We have averaged 75 psi air pressure, with very few events of low pressure over the past four months. We have been able to run with one compressor offline for more than months now. **At times, we have run with two compressors offline for several days. We are working on some automation changes to manage our big users to make this permanent.**

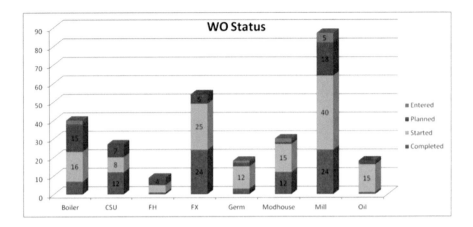

We continue to excel in the scheduling and planning of leak work orders. Only 22% of all WOs are in the planning or planned phase. **We have either started or completed 78% of all leaks that have been tagged!**

**Much recognition continues to be given to the planners and maintenance coordinators for jumping on board with the process and getting the WOs planned and executed!

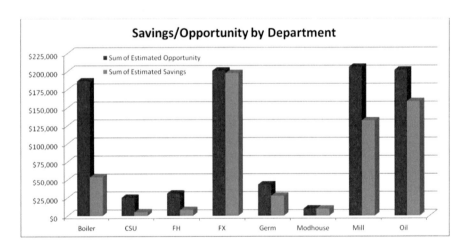

So where is the opportunity? Where is the money? We still have huge opportunities in WATER and AIR USAGE, which makes the idea of having two compressors offline very feasible. We are gaining ground on STEAM/ GAS leaks with several fixed in the Feedhouse and Boiler areas this month.

1. SDT: www.sdthearmore.com

2. UE Systems: www.uesystems.com

108

Case Study 2: Steam Traps

Inspection Notes & Report on
Steam Trap Inspection and Analysis

Inspection & Analysis: Hans De Kegel
Report: Ilse Van de Wiele

In this report you will find an exhaustive analysis of all steam traps, with notes on whether they are in good or bad condition, function poorly, or were out of use during the inspection.

You can also find a *Trap Health Report* in this report. This will give you a quick overview of the condition of each steam trap and/or of a specific zone in case the plant is divided into zones.

Hans De Kegel
European PdM Partners N.V.
Merelbeke, Belgium

1. Location of the steam traps

The steam traps were inspected on **22 & 23 December 2009, 6 & 7 January 2010**, and **1 & 2 February 2010**. Each steam trap has a unique number that corresponds with a location in the plant.

For example:

FIL-00090 is steam trap 90 in department FIL

KA-00010 is steam trap 10 in department KA

B6030 is a steam trap from building 6030

T5090 is a steam trap from area T

2. Overview of the charts and lists

For this survey, we have divided everything into the following zones:
- Thermal Power Station
- General Services
- Cold Department
- Hot Department
- Conditioning
- Testing
- Filtration
- Warehouses

In the typical survey report, each zone would include a number of details, such as:

• A list of all technical data of the different steam traps:	annex 1
• A list of location of the steam traps:	annex 2
• A list of measuring results of each steam trap:	annex 3
• List of steam traps to be inspected:	annex 4
• List of steam traps to be replaced:	annex 5
• All steam traps in numbers:	annex 6

This survey report was condensed to show examples of the above for this case study.

For each zone you will find a survey with observations on steam traps, other matters and a Trap Health Report.

In this report, you will find several Trap Health Reports.

The reports give a *quick overview* of the condition of all steam traps. To keep this overview graphically simple, the reports have been divided into 4 different colors: Green, Yellow, Red, and Blue.

Green	**The steam trap has no problem. Steam trap is not in an alarming condition.**
Yellow	**The steam trap has a temperature problem.**
Red	**There is a manifest problem with the steam trap.**
Blue	**The Steam trap is not in use during inspection.**

In addition, the Trap Health Reports are subdivided into the sections *Inspection*, *Visual*, *Total*, and *Previous*.

Inspection is the measurement itself and its analysis.

Visual means the condition on visual inspection and control. Can be an external leak, turn cock, in front of or behind with leakage of spindle or flange.

Previous is the state during a previous measurement.

Total gives the real outcome of both *Inspection* and *Visual*.

For example:

Trap ID	Inspection	Visual	Total	Previous
AOS-Z-001				
AOS-Z-002				
AOS-Z-01A				
AOS-Z-02A				

In this example, steam trap AOS-Z-001, on general inspection, was found to be in yellow (temperature problem); the visual inspection was all right and hence green. The total column indicates that the overall situation remains yellow because there is a possible problem.

For steam trap AOS-Z-002, we see that there is a problem. While visually one cannot see anything wrong during the inspection, the final result is red, which means there is a serious problem.

111

Steam trap AOS-Z-02A was found to be in a "blue" condition, meaning the steam trap is not in use. The Visual result is red, meaning there may be an external problem, like a steam trap that is fitted incorrectly by 90°.

3. Codes and abbreviations used in this report

3.1 Use

Drip	Draining of steam pipe
Proc	Steam trap is used for processing
TRCR	Steam trap is used for tracing
HEAT	Steam trap is used for heating, e.g. rooms

3.2 Fitting

O-LW	Fitted outside less than two meters above ground level
O-HG	Fitted outside higher than two meters above ground level
I-LW	Fitted inside less than two meters above ground level
I-HG	Fitted inside higher than two meters above ground level

3.3 Recycling

YES	Condensate is being recycled
NO	Condensate is not recycled

3.4 Operation

CTU	Steam trap is in service continuously
RV	Steam trap is in service continuously but pressure can fluctuate because of adjustable valve
BATCH	Steam trap is operating within a batch system

3.5 Type

DISC	Thermodynamic steam trap
THERMO	Thermostatic steam trap
TEMP ADJ	Adjustable thermostatic steam trap
FLOAT	Float steam trap
BUCKET	Reversed bucket steam trap
OTHER	Other

3.6 Test result

Good	Measurement results are good, steam trap OK and no problems
Leak/s	Small leak with loss of steam
Leak/m	Medium leak with loss of steam
Leak/l	Large steam leak
Blowing	Valve of steam trap is blowing
L/Body	Leak to the body of steam trap, through the housing
Blocked	Steam trap is blocked; neither condensate nor steam can flow through
Not in S	Steam trap not in service
No Check	Steam trap not checked
Low Temp	Temperature of steam trap too low in relation to its front pressure or adjustment

4. Measuring results

422 steam traps have been measured of a total of **476**

- Steam traps not in service: 54
- Steam traps that were not checked: 0

Total number of steam traps in a good condition (checked): 312

Total number of steam traps that are blowing through: 4

Total number of leaking steam traps: 30

Total number of blocked steam traps: 61

Number of steam traps below operation temperature: 16

5. Description of measurement results

5.1. Blowing steam traps

In this case, the discharge valve of the steam trap remains released and does not close anymore. Because the steam trap remains open, condensate and steam in large flows are being evacuated. In this case a steam trap is blowing. The condensate is not kept inside and the system will work on a maximum capacity together, while a large quantity of steam is being lost. Although a blowing steam trap will not have a negative influence on the production itself, it has to be repaired because of the continuous, huge, and expensive energy loss. There could be several reasons why a steam trap is blowing. For instance, between the valve and the valve basis there could be strange particulates, some parts could be damaged, etc. If, in addition, this blowing steam trap is connected to a network of mains that, because of the damage, are losing their condensate, the consequence of the blowing steam trap will be that in this condensate main the counter-pressure will be too high, which will result in more negative consequences for the other steam traps that are connected to the same condensate main.

5.2. Blocked steam traps

Steam traps are blocked when the escape valve of the steam trap is not released. Since the steam trap remains closed, no condensate will be drained. If condensate is being stopped, it will fill nearly the whole steam space of the steam system that causes the heating capacity to drop markedly. Blocking is a serious problem because it will have direct effects on the production capacity of the system.

5.3. Leaking steam traps

From the point of view of energy saving, steam loss is the second problem, after blowing steam traps. The cause of steam loss can be divided into the three following groups:

- Steam loss in closed position.
- Steam loss while blowing off condensate.
- Steam loss due to a valve that closes too slowly.

As a general rule we can conclude that bad functioning of steam traps and steam loss are being caused by insufficient maintenance, broken-down valves and valve bases, or incorrect adjustment of thermostatic steam traps.

6. Summary of the measurements

We calculated a yearly loss of **59.685,79€**. This equals a loss of **2436,15** tons each year. For our calculations, we used the cost of **24,50€** per ton of steam.

We have prepared lists for each zone in which steam traps should be checked and have detailed which steam traps have to be replaced and where each of them can be found.

7. Observations

Remarks on the Thermal Power Station Zone

The steam traps described here are in the tunnel from the stairs by Conditioning:

Steam trap TC-30130 - There's a leak at the connection with the pipe of this steam trap. It is a bit harder to find, as it is hidden right behind the insulation and the pipe.

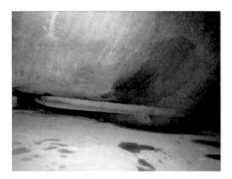

Steam trap TC-30110 - There's a leak close by this steam trap in the pipe where condensate runs through. The leak has temporarily been closed off with a piece of rubber. It would be best to find a permanent solution that handles the leak before it gets any worse and before hot condensate flies all around.

This picture was taken in the basement of the Thermal Power Station, at the level of steam traps TC-10060 and TC-10061.

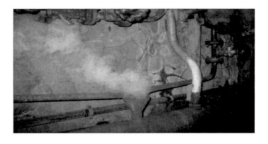

This diagram shows what is going wrong:

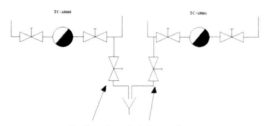

Both valves let steam by.
Although closed, they let steam escape.

Steam trap TC-30220 – There are two problems with this steam trap. One has to do with the connection of the steam trap. The other has to do with its environment.

First, the connection of the steam trap with its draining point is not correct. Draining a steam pipe can be done in different ways. In general, we can assume that a complete draining system consists of:

• A collection bucket composed of a thick pipe part;
• Two valves, one in front and one behind the steam trap;
• One filter;
• One steam trap; and
• One bypass.

Here you see a few examples, showing the best way to install the drain:

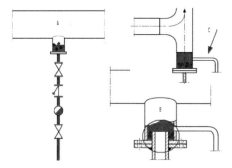

The way steam trap TL-30220 has been fitted, all the dirt will flow to the steam trap for two reasons:

1. There is no filter.

2. The condensate pipe is fitted underneath the condensate collector, as shown in figure A. Either a filter should be added or the fitting should configured as in figure B, or preferably as shown in figure C.

Note that the steam trap cannot be fitted too closely on to the steam pipe. Look at the following schematic drawing for reference:

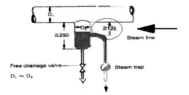

The second problem with this steam trap is the insulation of the steam pipes it should be draining. In some spots in the plant, there are quite a few badly insulated pipes; some are even missing insulation. See the preceding photo for an example.

Please note that though we have commented on the condition of some steam pipes we did not check all steam pipes, and we instead concentrated on the steam traps and condensate problems.

There are plenty of cases where exchange of heat plays a role. In every boiler, condenser, air heater, heat exchanger, etc., heat is being transferred from one medium to another. The transfer of heat can happen in three different ways:

- By conductivity,

- By convection (moving of particles in a liquid or gaseous medium), or

- By radiation (transfer of heat between two bodies that aren't connected).

A precondition for any of the three to happen is the existence of a temperature difference. As long as this condition is fulfilled, heat will flow from the place with higher temperature towards a place of lower temperature.

We have heat conduction through an even wall and heat conduction through a pipe wall.

When we have a thick-walled tube with an inside radius r_1 and outside radius r_2, with heat temperatures T_1 at the outside and T_2 on the inside, if $T_1 > T_2$, the heat will flow from inside out, whereby the surface to be overcome becomes greater and greater.

In calculating the heat flow (ϕ) the following formula can be used.

$$\phi = (2\Pi \cdot r_m \, (T_1 - T_2)) \, / \, (\delta / \lambda)$$

T_1 = temperature of the outside wall of the pipe in K

T_2 = temperature at the outside wall of the pipe in K

δ = $r_2 - r_1$ (thickness of the wall in meters)

λ = wavelength heat conduction coefficient (in W/m K)

r_m = medium radius

As an example, I have calculated the cost of a steam pipe that has not been lagged over a distance of 33'7". The steam pipe has a diameter of 1" or 25 mm, an inside temperature of 150°C (302 °F) (120°C when this pipe is correctly lagged with a thickness of 1/8" insulation), and an outside temperature of 20°C (68°F). The price of 10^6 Kj is £1,15, and the pipe is in use for 300 days. Without knowing the exact kind of pipe material used, but assuming 50 W/m K, which corresponds to cast iron with a bit more carbon, the insulation value is then equal to 0,02 W/m K.

When the steam pipe is used without proper lagging, the consumption is equal to **3.610 J/ms**.

When the pipe is insulated the heat flow (Φ) is equal to **13,7 J/ms**, which gives a saving of 3.610 − 13,7 = 3.596,3 J/ms. In real money on a yearly basis this is equal to 3.596,3 x 300 x 24 x 3600 x 100 / 10^9) x £1,15 = **14.880 euro** each year for a steam pipe of 25mm or 1".

Consider the following information about losses. We did not make an inventory of what was and what was not insulated when it comes to valves and flanges, but this gives you an idea of how much loss is possible.

Energy recuperation by insulation of valves and flanges

On the next page you'll find a calculation example we made a year ago of the cost of loss at a valve and a flange under different pressures.

Basic principles are:

- Ambient temperature of 25 °C
- Number of days steam is on equals 365

Losses per flange are:

Pressure		DN50	DN65	DN80	DN100	DN125	DN150	DN200
1 bar	kWh/year	564	728	854	1109	1364	1650	2147
	Tons of steam/year	0,83	1,07	1,25	1,63	2,00	2,42	3,15
5 bar	kWh/year	1398	1803	2116	2747	3378	4086	5317
	Tons of steam/year	1,98	2,56	3,00	3,89	4,79	5,79	7,54
9 bar	kWh/year	1736	2239	2627	3411	4194	5073	6602
	Tons of steam/year	2,44	3,14	3,69	4,79	5,89	7,12	9,27
16 bar	kWh/year	2182	2815	3304	4289	5274	6379	8301
	Tons of steam/year	3,04	3,93	4,61	5,98	7,35	8,89	11,57
21 bar	kWh/year	2397	3092	3628	4710	5792	7006	9117
	Tons of steam/year	3,33	4,30	5,04	6,55	8,05	9,74	12,67

Losses for each valve are:

Pressure		DN50	DN65	DN80	DN100	DN125	DN150	DN200
1 bar	kWh/year	1.147	1.479	1.736	2.253	2.771	3.351	4.361
	Tons of steam/year	1,68	2,17	2,55	3,31	4,07	4,92	6,40
5 bar	kWh/year	2.840	3.663	4.298	5.580	6.862	8.300	10.801
	Tons of steam/year	4,02	5,19	6,08	7,90	9,71	11,75	15,29
9 bar	kWh/year	3.526	4.548	5.337	6.928	8.519	10.305	13.410
	Tons of steam/year	4,951135	6,386205	7,494102	9,728151	11,9622	14,47006	18,83004
16 bar	kWh/year	4.433	5.718	6.711	8.712	10.713	12.958	16.862
	Tons of steam/year	6,18	7,97	9,36	12,15	14,94	18,07	23,51
21 bar	kWh/year	4.869	6.280	7.370	9.568	11.766	14.231	18.520
	Tons of steam/year	6,77	8,73	10,25	13,30	16,36	19,79	25,75

Diagram:

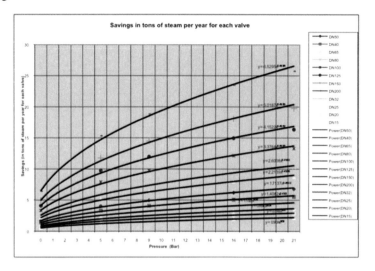

Remarks on the General Services Zone

Steam trap AD-1010 - The steam trap below is mounted 90° incorrectly. This is why this steam trap blows through. It would be best to mount it again, this time correctly, as indicated in the following diagram. We also found a leak on the filter of this steam trap that needs to be fixed.

The correct mounting is as follows:

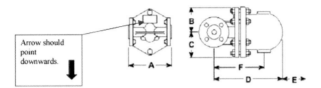

Arrow should point downwards.

This float steam trap by Spirax Sarco has two arrows on its body. One indicates the flow of the condensate, which in this steam trap is correctly done. A second arrow indicates the direction in which the float has been fitted in the steam trap. Here it should point downwards, so it should be turned 90°.

Steam trap AD-1020 – This trap has the same problem: it's mounted 90° incorrectly, and it should be fixed according to the explanation above.

With this steam trap one can also see a pipe that is not insulated (see the following picture). The problems caused by uninsulated pipes can be found in the remarks regarding the Thermal Power Plant.

Remarks on the Cold Department Zone

Steam trap KA-3000 - The valve for this steam trap is closed. Draining is thus not possible. If no draining occurs because of a blocked steam trap, and condensate cannot go through, there is a fair chance of getting:

a. Non-flowing water.

b. Wet steam.

Several problems are possible with non-moving water, including corrosion and deposits of impurities.

The following photos were taken of a steam pipe that had a steam trap mounted to the end of it.

Erosion-corrosion is a process that frequently occurs in liquid transport systems.

Erosion-corrosion can be defined as the damaging of a metal that goes faster and faster through a combination of erosion and corrosion, when affected by a fast moving liquid. The metal can thus be scraped off as solid particles or, in case of a strong erosion-corrosion, as dissolved ions. Metals that build up a protective layer against corrosion from themselves are especially very sensitive for this. Because of the abrasive effect of the high velocity of the liquid, the protective layer is made to disappear.

Even with a small amount of corrosion of the medium, the damage can increase a lot in a short period of time through a synergy of high velocity and turbulence of the liquid. Solid particles or gas bubbles in the liquid increase the effect even more.

The degree of erosion-corrosion is dependent on two factors: the velocity and the corrosiveness of the medium. Too high a velocity causes turbulence in the liquid, which causes erosion to go faster. Also, obstructions in the stream can cause turbulence and local erosion-corrosion damage (see the following photo).

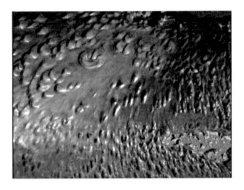

T-pieces, curves, elbow joints, pumps, and seals, for example, are very sensitive locations. Also, entrances and exits of the pipes in a heat exchanger, sudden changes in diameter, incorrect welding, and deposits have to be monitored for these problems. Depending on the metal and the medium, there is no erosion-corrosion with certain velocities. Concerning the corrosiveness of the medium, however, we can say that even a small amount of corrosiveness in combination with some turbulence can cause damage. Increased possibility for damage comes also from the presence of solid particles (sand) or gas bubbles in the liquid (see the following photo).

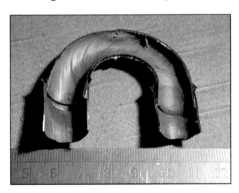

In addition to the problem with the valve, there is also a heat exchanger with steam trap **KA-3000** that has many leaks (see the following pictures).

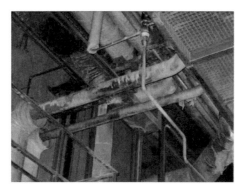

On the third floor of the Cold Department, above the heat exchangers, there are many steam pipes that are not insulated. We showed in the section on the Thermal Power Station that this costs a lot of money. It would be best to reinsulate these pipes or repair the existing insulation.

Steam trap KA-01031 - This trap has a leak before the attachment under the tank.

Remarks on the Hot Department Zone

Steam trap WA-145 - This steam trap has a mechanism to get rid of water. One can do this through manual operation, by pushing the hand purging knob. With this specific steam trap, this knob is stuck.

Steam trap WA-208 - This steam trap is mounted incorrectly in the same manner as steam trap TC-30220. Here, one cannot easily get rid of the water through the steam trap because of the velocity of the steam. If there is condensate (water) in the pipe, it moves past the point where the water can go out because the condensate goes along with the steam velocity.

 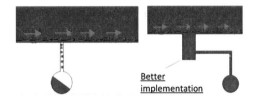

Better
implementation

Steam trap WA-404 - Inside this steam trap, the spring of the manual operation is broken.

Steam trap WA-406 - The operation is broken on this steam trap.

Steam trap WA-408 - This steam trap has the same problems as steam trap WA-208.

Steam traps WA-504, WA-505, WA-506, WA-507, WA-604, WA-605, WA-606, and WA-607 - All manual operations with these steam traps are blocked. Getting rid of the extra water is thus not possible.

Steam trap WA-708 - This steam trap has the same problems as steam trap WA-208.

In the CIP kitchen, many of the stopcocks are not insulated:
3xDN200 • 1xDN150 • 2xDN100 • 2xDN50 • 1xDN25
Together, this amounts to a loss of 77,6 Tons/year.

Also, it would be best to place back the insulation that used to be there. This is a situation at the level of the steam traps WA-20100 and WA-20110.

European PdM Partners nv also has a lot of experience with other techniques, such as vibration analysis, thermographic or infrared checkups, ultrasound, and Motor Current analysis.

We also found the following problems with the pumps in this zone:

• Pump BE04312170 PUM 200000: the rubber coupling blocks are worn out.

• Pump BE04312170 PUM 210000: there is a misalignment between motor and the pump.

• Pump BE04312170 PUM 080000: the bearings of the motor are breaking down.

• Pump CD312102 MOT 07.04.01: We suspect a misalignment.

At the level of Line 3, MAKO 1 – The insulation is totally gone. The problems with lack of insulation can be found in the remarks regarding the Thermal Power Station.

On top of the platform next to the condensate tank CD31260 CRT 01.00.00, there is a leak by a flange of a stopcock (see the following picture).

Steam trap WA-20090 – The bolt has loosened on the flange before the steam trap. It should be tightened again before a leak through the seal starts. Also, this trap is extraneous and could be removed.

As you can see in the diagram, there are two steam traps to get rid of the water. One should be sufficient. There is also a bypass. Therefore, steam trap WA-20090 can be eliminated.

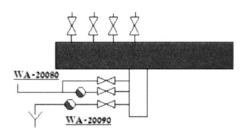

The insulation on the same steam dispenser needs to be replaced, as mentioned above (see the following photo). It is simply on the ground next to the dispenser. To give you an idea of the amount of loss in heat and energy, please take a look at the diagram in the remarks concerning the Thermal Power Station.

At the level of CD 312102 – There is a leak on the pipe. Water is coming from the insulation.

Steam trap WA-20050 - This steam trap is mounted upside down. When a steam trap is mounted upside down, dirt gets into the bottom of the steam trap. That is where the bi-metals are located that ensure the working of the steam trap. If dirt gets between these bi-metals, the working gets disturbed and the steam trap starts leaking. It would be best to place it back the right way, i.e. turn it 180°.

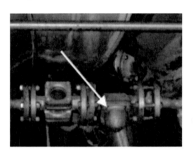
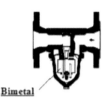

Bimetal

Remarks on the Conditioning Zone

Bottle line 3

Steam trap **CD-F3050** is insulated. It is not a good idea to keep it that way, for the following reasons:

- Thermostatic steam traps only take away the water after the temperature of the condensate has gone down a few degrees below the steam temperature. If the heat of the condensate does not dissipate fast enough, the condensate is kept inside unnecessarily long, and that can eventually cause water hammer and loss of output.

- Closed float steam traps usually contain a thermostatic ventilator that for the same reason can cause problems when these steam traps are insulated.

- Bucket steam traps are supposed to lose heat into the environment so that steam that is locked inside the bucket can condensate. That then causes the valve to open again, so that newly formed condensate again can be gotten rid of. If the steam in the bucket cannot condensate (because of loss of heat), then the steam trap would, theoretically, remain closed permanently.

- Thermodynamic steam traps function badly when the revaporisation steam under the cover disappears through condensation. Again, this is only possible when the steam trap does not get insulated.

Building 3

Close to pump BE03 313103 EPP 80.61.01 – The procedure attached and shown in the picture (Procedure 4815 ELP open taps) is correct. However, we can handle this simply by mounting a steam trap just before the stop cock (see diagram).

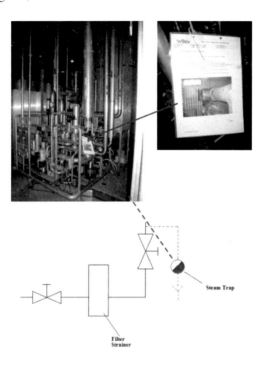

Building 4

Steam Trap CD-F6072 – This steam trap is mounted incorrectly by 90°. See the remarks regarding the General Services zone for instructions on how to mount it correctly.

Building 5

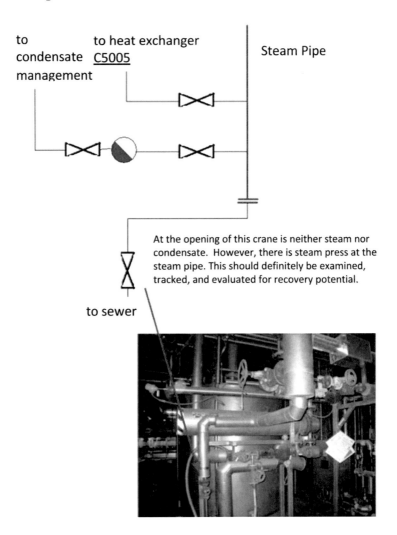

to
condensate
management

to heat exchanger
C5005

Steam Pipe

to sewer

At the opening of this crane is neither steam nor condensate. However, there is steam press at the steam pipe. This should definitely be examined, tracked, and evaluated for recovery potential.

This photo shows a globe valve next to Building 5 that is constantly open, causing a plain loss of steam. We have left it open because we do not know the reason why it was opened. It should be checked and, if possible, closed.

Steam Trap CD-F5036 – There is a leak on the one-way valve in this steam trap. The gasket should be replaced.

Building 6

Steam Trap CD-F6045 - The connection should be on the bottom, not on the side.

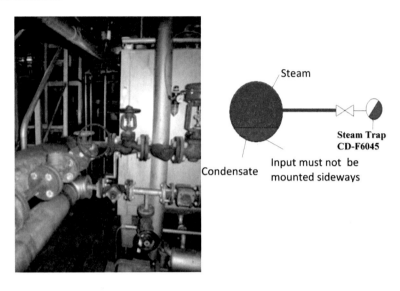

Steam Trap CD-F6030 - This steam trap is mounted 180° incorrectly. Explanation on how to mount it correctly can be found in the remarks regarding the General Services Zone.

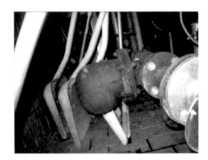

Trap Line 5

Steam Trap CD-V5150 - This steam trap is mounted correctly. Just before the steam trap, a one-way valve is mounted. These valves can be mounted before or after the steam trap, for two reasons:

1. Before the steam trap, if one suspects that there will be a vacuum in the pipe before the condenspot, when one closes down the installation.

2. After a steam trap, because one can expect a certain back pressure.

In this case, it would be best to mount the valve **AFTER** the steam trap and **NOT** before.

Remarks on the Testing (PF) Zone

In the test area, at the end of the pipe, it would be best to place a steam trap. Without it you have a large part of non-moving water, which can cause water hammer, in addition to other disadvantages non-moving water can cause (see the remarks regarding the Cold Department zone for a description of these problems)

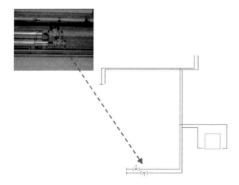

Remarks on the Filtration Zone

Three steam traps, **FIL-0012**, **FIL-0022,** and **FIL-0032,** are all mounted 90° incorrectly (see the following pictures).

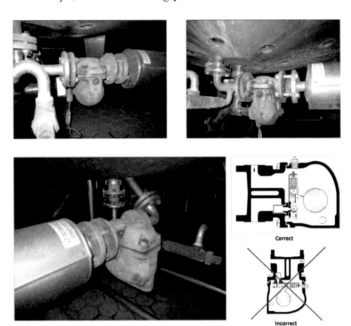

In the filtration area, there are large heat exchangers. One of them leaks when we start using it (see the following picture).

Remarks on the Warehouses (VW) Zone

Steam trap VW-10280 - This steam trap is mounted 90° incorrectly. This float steam trap of Spirax Sarco has 2 arrows on the main body. One shows the direction the condensate stream follows. This is correct with this steam trap. The second arrow shows the direction of how the float is mounted in the steam trap. This should point downwards in this case, so the steam trap should be turned over 90°.

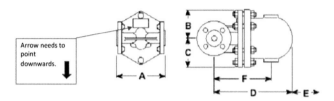

Steam trap VW-11090

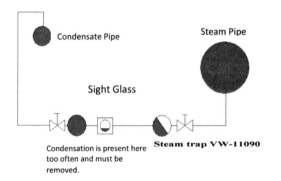

Steam trap VW-11090

Steam trap VW-11091 - The steam pipe "hangs" down. This should be fixed before the pipe comes down any more and breaks.

8. Additional information

Detecting defects and their causes can be done in different ways. Here you'll find a short summary and terms used during the analysis.

The defects and steam traps are divided into four groups: blocking, blowing steam traps, leaking steam traps, and insufficient drainage. Here we'll deal with finding the causes, based on the symptoms.

A steam trap that isn't working well is not always defective. If a defective steam trap is located, it does not have to be removed automatically. One should first check the production conditions, which may avoid unnecessary disassembling.

The preliminary checking up consists of:

1. Identification of the symptoms. Find which of the four above symptoms occur. This is the starting point for detecting a malfunction.
2. Check the temperature of the steam trap.
3. Notice the type, model, and operation life of the steam trap. Check if the steam trap is appropriate for the application and the given plant circumstances. (pressure temperature, capacity, etc.). Check the operation time of the steam trap.
4. Have a close look at the overall installation. Have the supply and drainage pipes correctly been connected? Has the supply of condensate under gravity been considered? Is the steam trap situated downstream of the point of drainage? Has the steam trap been dimensioned correctly? Is the diameter of the pipe equal to the diameter of the steam trap? Is the drainage pipe one size bigger than the steam trap if this pipe is longer than three meters? Has each user got its own steam trap?
5. Have the valves upstream and downstream of the steam trap been completely opened?
6. Has the bypass valve been securely closed, and is it not leaking? Check the bypass valve and close the valves upstream and downstream of the steam trap.
7. If a blow off valve has been installed downstream of the steam trap, check to see if it is securely closed.
8. Is the steam pressure normal?
9. Is the value of the counter pressure normal?
10. How high is the temperature of the drained condensate?

Next consider the following important questions:

1. Does the defect occur gradually or at once?
2. How did the steam trap function at the time of starting up?
3. Is the piping old or new? Have the pipes been renewed recently?
4. Have there ever been water hammer pulses?

Blocking

First check the supplied steam. Check to see if the air cocks before and after the steam traps are open.

For mechanical steam traps, check to see if the front pressure and the difference in pressure fall within the permitted values.

If the steam trap is warmed up, it is almost certain there is an accumulation of steam This can be checked in this way:

a. Is the steam equipment easily liable to steam accumulation? (cylinder drier)
b. Can the condensate float under gravity?
c. Open the bypass valve or pour cold water on the piping downstream of the steam trap and onto the steam trap itself. If the blockage is moved, it certainly was an accumulation of steam.

When the steam trap is cold, different causes are possible. First and foremost check to see if the condensate is released. If no condensate drains away when opening the link at the intake, the piping is blocked. If condensate is drained, open the blowing valve of the steam trap. If no condensate can be drained there, the filter is blocked. Steam traps installed on new pipes may after some time become obstructed with dirt and sand.

When the condensate flows away through the blowing valve, the blockage is situated upstream and downstream of the valve. Sometimes the blockage is caused by the sealer used to seal off the threads on the fittings.

Depending on the type of steam trap, there may be different causes for the blockage

- Float filled with water (float steam trap)
- Worn out seat (bucket steam trap)
- Loose inner cap or leak through the inner sealing (thermodynamic steam trap with steam housing)

Those causes can only be found by disassembling the steam trap.

Blowing steam traps

The following questions are important for blowing steam traps:

1. Is the capacity of the steam trap in proportion to the supply of condensate?

2. With thermodynamic steam traps the following things should be checked:

   a. If the front pressure is higher than 0,6 bar the counter pressure must be lower than half the front pressure. If the front pressure is lower than 0,6 bar, the difference in pressure must be higher than 0,3 bar.

   b. Check the possibilities of rising counter pressure. For example, drainage towards a common collector, too small a collector or pressure variations within the condensate drainage pipes.

3. Can fluid hammer occur? Heavy fluid hammer can bend levers or compress the float of a mechanical steam trap, resulting in the steam trap leaking steam. In case of a free floating float steam trap, the float is protected by a fluid hammer housing.

4. If the cause of blowing cannot be detected in this way, parts of the steam trap can be damaged or its inner wall can be pierced.

Blowing easily happens if a valve is worn down due to the long and uninterrupted use of the steam trap or because of jamming of odd particles after the replacement or renewal of the piping system.

A piercing of the inner wall often occurs with thermodynamic steam traps when they are undersized.

Leaking steam traps

Loss of steam is mostly reflected in percentages of weight with regard to the drained condensate (more exactly the mix of steam and condensate). Generally, the loss of steam goes up together with the higher supply of condensate in thermodynamic steam traps, and the loss of steam drops with a higher supply of condensate in float steam traps.

That is why, when considering the reasons of steam loss, one should also take into consideration the supply of condensate. Most steam traps are used for medium-sized supply of condensate in accordance with their capacity. Steam traps that are being used to drain pipes often function under really limited pressure.

Common causes of steam loss are:

a. Worn valve and valve seat.

b. Defects at the surface of the valve and valve seat.

c. Odd particles that are being trapped between valve and valve seat. Fibrous particles are difficult to blow off.

d. Valve and valve seat are covered with a greasy film.

Loss of steam in thermodynamic steam traps is always accompanied by a shortened cycle. A short frequency cycle indicates the degree of wearing. Rattling steam traps must be taken down immediately and repaired. Rattling often occurs in steam traps with natural cooling. In steam traps with interchangeable inner mechanisms, steam can directly leak through towards the outlet because the seal between the housing and the valve seat is damaged.

Mechanical steam traps are usually equipped with a manual or automatic air vent. This air vent valve sometimes leaks due to wearing.

Steam traps with a free-floating float do not lose steam during the normal functioning because the seat is situated below the level of condensate. Those steam traps will only leak steam if there are bends in the surface of the float that touch the seat. If the float doesn't rest upon the damaged part of the seat, the leakage of steam automatically stops.

Insufficient drainage

First, check to see if the steam trap is suitable for its application. Does the capacity of the steam trap correspond with the supply of condensate?

Second, find the answer to the following questions: Can the steam equipment itself or the supply pipes of the condensate cause steam blockage? Does steam blockage often occur? Do the front pressure, the counter pressure, and the difference pressure correspond to the specified values?

Dirt in filter elements or supply and drainage pipes may be the causes. When, at the start, the capacity of the steam traps has become too small, dirt is the most probable reason.

Figures

Test Results		Previous
Good	312	193
Blocked	61	47
Small leak	7	1
Medium leak	16	2
Large leak	6	1
Blowing	4	1
Leak Body	0	2
Total	94	54
Low temperature	16	24
Measured in total	422	271
Not checked	0	1
Not in service	54	204
Total	54	205
Total	476	476

Brand	
Gestra	162
Spirax	300
AWH	7
Steamtech	1
Armstrong	4
TLV	2
Niagara	0
Velan	0
Blok	0
Byvap	0
total	476

Type	
Float	312
Thermo	114
Bucket	42
Orifice	1
Disc	7
total	476

Application	
Drip	164
Proces	233
Dryer	0
Tracing	0
Heat	79
total	476

pressure	
0,5 - 3 bar	471
3,1 - 8 bar	5
8,1 - 12 bar	0
12,1 - 20 bar	0
20,1 - 80 bar	0
> 80,1 bar	0
total	476

144

Number of Traps by Zone	
General Services	24
Testing	157
Hot Department	148
Cold Department	24
Central Thermal	23
Pilot Brewery	11
Heating Department	73
Filtration	16
Total	476

Loss of Steam		Cost/ton	Total Cost	
		€ 24.50		
Kg/hour	332.13		0.5 - 3 bar	€ 59,685.79
Ton/year	2,436.15		3.1 - 8 bar	€ 0.00
Euro/year	€ 59,685.79		8.1 - 12 bar	€ 0.00
			12.1 - 20 bar	€ 0.00
General Services	€ 6,597.92		20.1 - 80 bar	€ 0.00
Testing	€ 30,974.03		> 80.1 bar	€ 0.00
Hot Department	€ 3,787.29			
Cold Department	€ 0.00			
Central Thermal	€ 5,797.61			
Pilot Brewery	€ 0.00			
Heating Department	€ 6,394.50			
Filtration	€ 6,134.45		**Total**	**€ 59,685.79**

Overview

Measuring results	Amount of steam traps	% Division
Good condition	312	65,55%
Too low temperature	16	3,36%
Small leak	7	1,47%
Medium leak	16	3,36%
Large leak	6	1,26%
Blowing	4	0,84%
Blocked	61	12,82%
Leak body	0	0,00%
Not checked	0	0,00%
Not in service	54	11,34%
Total	476	100%

Monetary Loss by Zone	
General Services	€ 6,597.92
Testing	€ 30,974.03
Warm Department	€ 3,787.29
Cold Department	€ 0.00
Central Thermal	€ 5,791.61
Pilot Brewery	€ 0.00
Heating Department	€ 6,394.50
Filtration	€ 6,134.45
Total:	€ 59,685.79

Total Trap Health Report

Inspection Results (measured and visual) by Zone				
General Services	13	1	6	4
Testing	94	5	29	29
Warm Department	109	9	24	6
Cold Department	13	0	1	10
Central Thermal	19	0	4	0
Pilot Brewery	6	0	0	5
Heating Department	43	1	29	0
Filtration	13	0	3	0
	310	16	96	54

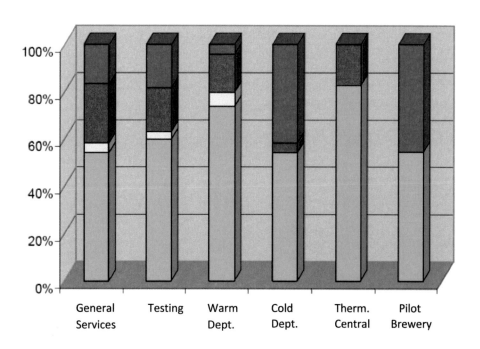

Sample Trap Health Report for Warm Department

Trap Health Report
Warm Department

	inspection	Visual	Total		Previous
Percentage of traps in green condition	59%	97%	58%		56%
Percentage of traps in yellow condition	6%	0%	6%		0%
Percentage of traps in red condition	14%	3%	16%		34%
Percentage of traps in Blue condition	20%	0%	20%		10%
Number of traps in Green condition	88	144	86		70
Number of traps in Yellow condition	9	0	9		0
Number of traps in Red condition	21	4	23		43
Number of traps in Blue condition	30	0	30		13
Total traps Count In Program	148	148	148		126
Total traps Collected This inspection	118	148	118		113

Trap ID	inspection	Visual	Total		Previous
WA-00010					
WA-00020					
WA-00030					
WA-00040					
WA-00050					
WA-00060					
WA-00070					
WA-00080					
WA-00100					
WA-00101					
WA-00102					
WA-00103					
WA-00104					
WA-00105					
WA-00106					
WA-00107					
WA-00108					
WA-00109					
WA-00120					
WA-00121					
WA-00122					
WA-00123					
WA-00124					
WA-00125					
WA-00130					
WA-00131					

Chapter 12

Reliability and Energy, the Allied Way

Introduction

Allied Reliability Inc. was founded in 1997 and began providing reliability services to the marketplace. Over the past 12 years, Allied has expanded its service footprint and has become one of the largest consulting, engineering, training, and service firms focused on predictive and preventive maintenance.

Allied helps companies build wealth and competitive advantage through world-class predictive maintenance and reliability across a global manufacturing network. Allied is the industry leader in designing and implementing a customized, integrated approach for identifying defects in assets utilizing predictive maintenance (PdM) and condition monitoring (CBM) services.

Our experience shows us that equipment reliability and energy efficiency go hand in hand.

Our experience shows us that equipment reliability and energy efficiency go hand in hand. The ability to understand how and why equipment fails is essential in understanding and developing energy-efficient strategies for the operation and maintenance of industrial equipment.

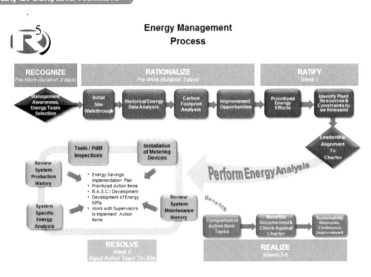

Process Overview

Allied incorporates an improvement approach called the (R⁵) Rapid Improvement Process. Its design and methodology is used to help our clients identify, achieve, and sustain improvement gains in reliability. The FIVE phases—Recognize, Rationalize, Ratify, Resolve, and Realize—closely resemble the DMAIC process.

Allied knows how to successfully integrate common PdM technologies to capture significant energy savings. We provide real-world strategies and solutions to maximize energy efficiency by providing hands-on tools and resources for reducing energy consumption, its related environmental impacts (carbon footprints), and improving overall equipment effectiveness (OEE) in industrial manufacturing environments.

1. Recognize Phase

- **Management Training:** As with all new efforts, it is critical that clear understanding of the objectives, expectations, and communication plan begins with the management team and filters through the organization. For an energy management program to be successful, it needs the commitment and support of the organization's management and should be in synergy with the organization's objectives.

  Since a common element of a successful energy management program is leadership commitment, a Fundamentals of Energy Management workshop will be conducted with select management and leadership team members, union leadership (if applicable), and key stakeholders. The goal is that each participant will learn the foundation of energy management and how best practice organizations select, implement, and sustain energy savings initiatives.

These activities well help create awareness and the desire to set the stage for cultural change that must occur within the organization as we move further into the energy management program. Clear objectives and goals of the program are developed during this session and will become the guiding principles of the site's energy management program.

Allied weaves Change Management into everything we do to help ensure tangible and sustainable results. This step is important in helping communicate all efforts and address any potential concerns. Coaching and mentoring will be provided to integrate the expectations with your organization's culture.

- **Energy Team Selection/Resource Allocation:** Energy management requires a systematic approach for selection of a suitable team to achieving and maintaining energy savings. The right people with the right attitude and motivation are instrumental to all successful initiatives.

  Selecting a team with the right skills and allocating the necessary required time to lead and execute the energy management program is extremely important. Allied will help facilitate the structure of the team that will have the overall responsibility for the program. In many cases, organizations may not have people with all the necessary technical expertise to implement each aspect of the energy management program. In such situations, Allied will support and provide resources to be engaged and carry out the required tasks.

  A cross-functional energy management team will be necessary for maximum sustainable improvements. Team members will be selected from the following areas of responsibility: plant management, engineering, finance, maintenance, procurement, and operations.

2. Rationalize Phase
- **Initial Plant Walkthrough:** Before beginning the energy analysis, we find it helpful to have some basic idea of the facility, the scope of the project, and the level of effort necessary to meet expectations.

The initial walkthrough will consist of a tour of the facility to visually inspect each of the energy-using systems along with the collection of energy consumption data. The building's energy costs and efficiency will be estimated through the analysis of energy bills and the brief survey of the facility.

This walkthrough will assist in identifying and providing savings and cost analysis of low-cost or no-cost measures.

Allied representatives will identify specific equipment that will be analyzed with PdM technologies during the analysis phase. An initial walkthrough assessment will highlight potential savings for the facility and therefore help to optimize available resources by being able to identify and prioritize areas or systems with the best potential for savings.

3. Ratify Phase

- **System Selection for Controlled Deployment:** Starting a new program or expanding an initiative often leads to many tasks needing to be completed with insufficient resources. Allied recognizes the need to prioritize efforts based on business impact and financial savings. We implement energy management programs in a way that pays for future rollout and minimizes the strain that can be applied to an organization attempting to tackle every opportunity at the same time.

  By prioritizing and selecting areas or systems upon which to focus efforts, we are able to create specialized teams with the expertise to evaluate, analyze, and identify real energy-saving solutions that can be implemented immediately.

  Some common systems for analysis include the following:

  - Compressed air systems
  - Compressed gas systems
  - Steam and hot water systems
  - Chillers
  - Cooling towers
  - Air handling units and air distribution systems
  - Pumping systems
  - Building electrical systems

- Lighting systems
- Process equipment

4. Resolve Phase

- **Perform Energy Analysis:** Once a system or area has been selected, Allied will assemble a team of experts to conduct an on-site energy analysis. An energy analysis consists of a detailed examination of how a facility uses energy, what the facility pays for that energy, and finally, a recommended program for changes in operating practices or energy-consuming equipment that will save money on energy bills.

  The analysis will assist in quantifying energy uses and losses through detailed review and analysis of equipment, systems, and operational characteristics. On-site testing and measurements are required during this step to ensure and quantify opportunities. Multiple tools and PdM technologies will be integrated to evaluate and capture significant energy savings and simplify ROI calculations.

  Tools and PdM technologies may include some of the following:

  - Power quality meter
  - Infrared thermography
  - Airborne ultrasonic
  - Data logger
  - Airflow measurement devices
  - Motor circuit analysis
  - Vibration analysis
  - Light meter

  The many steps in this analysis, including data gathering, observations, on-site interviews, data analysis, and developing the energy improvement plan, help to increase awareness throughout the organization of the impact energy can have on the business. Participation in the process facilitates organizational alignment as the future state becomes clearer, along with the stake each department/individual holds in the improvement process. This alignment is critical to the effective implementation of cultural and behavioral change associated with adopting energy management best practices.

- **Develop Energy Improvement Plan:** Once the analysis has been completed, energy-saving measures can be identified. The measures identified vary from one facility to another because of differences in equipment, system design, and operations. The energy improvement plan will provide a clear, straightforward explanation of the current situation, recommended improvements, and advantages of taking recommended actions. This energy improvement plan becomes the roadmap or strategy to address the gaps, or opportunities, identified from the analysis.

  The energy improvement plan will prioritize tasks addressing both criticality and maximum ROI. It is highly possible when utilizing PdM technologies during the analysis that defects of the equipment will be found. These results will be reported and may lead to non-energy-related benefits (i.e., scheduled repair prior to emergency breakdown repair).

5. Realize Phase

- **Implement Energy Improvement Plan:** Many are familiar with the typical assessment, analysis, reporting, and being left with hundreds of tasks to implement with no support or idea of how to accomplish them. This one fact is the graveyard of all initiatives. Allied believes that success comes only by implementing and changing the way we conduct business resulting in positive ROIs. We work hand in hand with your designated energy management team, providing them with the support, training, coaching, and mentoring to accomplish each of the recommended tasks.

  The completion of each task is critical to the success of the program. To make task implementation go as smoothly as possible, each task will have an implementation plan outlining:

  - What's needed
  - What's to be done (to-do's)
  - Who's responsible for each step
  - What's the deadline

  Anything less than this level of detail will slow or even derail the implementation process.

- **Measure and Verify Performance:** There is an old management adage that says, "You can't manage what you don't measure." In other words, unless you measure something, you will never know if it is getting better or worse. Savings can occur in the form of either repetitive, reoccurring savings or one-time savings. Recorded before and after, measurements are critical to eliminate the possibility of misrepresented or even unnoticed savings.

  Measurement systems will be put into place to collect data and express results as standard Key Performance Indicator (KPI) metrics. These metrics will be compared with benchmark data to help the organization evaluate and measure progress toward its defined goals. Integral inputs to the continuous improvement cycle are these energy management KPIs.

  It is important to communicate these metrics and the success of the program up and down the organization. People want to know how things are progressing and certainly like hearing the good news and how they are helping the organization become more efficient and environmentally responsible. With energy management metrics in place, your organization will begin to recognize the directly proportional relationship between equipment reliability and energy efficiency.

- **Training for Sustained Results:** Allied understands the key elements in sustaining positive results. The major elements we have discovered over the years involve impacting the entire organization's beliefs and behaviors related to energy management.

  Your organization must assume ownership of any improvement initiative, process, or program. To sustain culture change, everyone must be an active participant in the development and implementation.

  Beliefs are vital to the ability to change and must be modified prior to any behavior change. Education and knowledge transfer are keys to changing beliefs. Our model is to educate, followed by coaching and mentoring during implementation. In doing so, we help your people become self-sufficient by transferring the knowledge and ability to them.

  The most effective way to sustain change in your organization is to impact each and every level of the organization. Our model is tailored

155

to accomplish this, and our professionals are able to relate to individuals across multiple levels. By utilizing full-time employees trained in our model, we are able to deliver consistently and to effectively instill long-term successful and profitable change.

- **Continuous Improvement Cycle:** The moment you stop looking to improve is the moment you open yourself up to competitors making inroads as they find ways to improve quality or reduce costs. Perfection will never be achieved, and thus improvement is always possible.

The continuous improvement cycle is an effective team-involvement tool and forms the basis for a "lessons learned" database and best practices, which are continually reinforced at the leadership level and reflected in changed KPIs, updated business processes, and continual modeling and monitoring. Rigorous application of the continuous improvement cycle often realizes step change, while sharing lessons learned through a knowledge management system ensures that change is sustained, despite leadership changes or staff turnover issues.

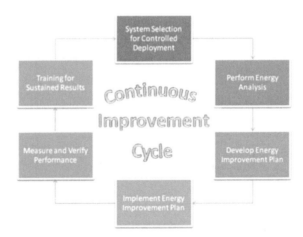

- **Reliability Based Process Flow:**

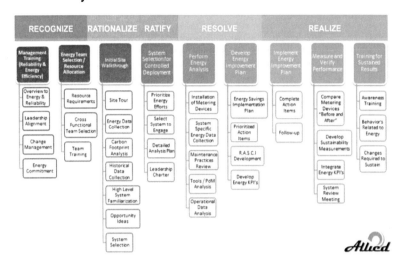

Allied Reliability, Inc.
4200 Faber Place Drive, Charleston, SC 29405
Tel: 843-414-5760 • Fax: 843-414-5779 • www.alliedreliability.com